THE  Holy Spirit AND YOU!

WORKING TOGETHER
AS HEAVEN'S 'DYNAMIC DUO'

RICK RENNER

Harrison House

The Holy Spirit and You:
Working Together as Heaven's Dynamic Duo
  (formerly *The Dynamic Duo*)
ISBN: 978-1-68031-143-3
Copyright © 2017 by Rick Renner
8316 E. 73rd St.
Tulsa, OK 74133

Published by Harrison House
Tulsa, OK 74133

2017 New Edition

Editorial Consultant: Cynthia Hansen
Text Design: Lisa Simpson, SimpsonProductions.net
Cover Design: Debbie Pullman, Zoe Life Creative Media,
  www.ZoeLifeCreative.com

DEDICATION

I lovingly dedicate this book
to all those whom the Lord used to lead me
to a fuller understanding
of the Holy Spirit.

CONTENTS

PREFACE

The book you hold in your hands right now carries the key to the mysteries of God, the power of God, the revelation of God's Word, and the fellowship of the Holy Spirit. It isn't so much the words I've written in this book that will transform you; it's the One I've written about. This book is about the Holy Spirit and His relationship with *you.*

Most Christians live and die never knowing the fellowship and companionship of the Holy Spirit. They have heard about the Holy Spirit and may even know doctrinal answers regarding the Third Person of the Godhead. But knowing *about* the Holy Spirit and personally knowing Him in daily fellowship are two very different things.

In the Early Church, there wasn't a New Testament for believers to turn to for direction, guidance, and answers. When believers assembled, there might be teaching or readings from the Old Testament or from an apostolic epistle. But for the most part, the early believers relied completely on the Holy Spirit. In the First Century, the Church experienced demonstrations of God's power, miracles, healings, mass evangelism, the full operation of the fivefold ministry gifts, and the gifts of the Spirit in amazing abundance.

We all look back to the Early Church in admiration, longing to see the power of God manifested at that level — and *beyond* that level — in our own generation.

Today we are privileged to have at our continual disposal not only the indwelling presence of the Holy Spirit, but also the Word of God — an invincible combination in the arsenal that the Bible calls "the weapons of our warfare" (*see* 2 Corinthians

10:4,5). Why, then, don't we see the same level of God's resurrection power and glory consistently manifested in our midst today that the Early Church experienced?

Although there may be many answers to this question, one answer is certain: Far too many Christians today have come to lean on their own understanding and intellectual abilities at the expense of consulting the Holy Spirit for His guidance in their lives. They assume they already know what He wants them to do. And because they don't depend on and yield to the leadership of the Holy Spirit the way the Early Church did, they miss opportunity after opportunity to see His power released in their lives.

> **Far too many Christians today have come to lean on their own understanding and intellectual abilities at the expense of consulting the Holy Spirit for His guidance in their lives.**

There is no substitute for the Word of God — for the true power of the Gospel (*see* Romans 1:16). But neither is there a substitute for the supernatural work of the Holy Spirit in the Church. In fact, these two go together as one. If the Spirit's presence and power are removed, all that's left is orthodoxy and religious works. But religion will never raise the dead, cast out demons, heal the sick, or turn cities and nations to Jesus Christ!

In my own life and ministry, I continue to learn more clearly every day how imperative it is for me to maintain intimacy and moment-by-moment communication with the Holy Spirit, no matter how knowledgeable I am of God's Word. If I hadn't cultivated a rich, solid relationship with the Holy Spirit during my early years of traveling in ministry throughout the United States, I would have been extremely skeptical, and may have even disobeyed Him, when He called me to move with my family to the former Soviet Union.

Without the help, guidance, and comfort of the Holy Spirit, Denise and I have no doubt that we would have become spiritual casualties at many junctures in our journey during those early years when we lived in Latvia and traveled throughout the former Soviet Union. Furthermore, we've stood and watched in awe as His power has moved through our ministry to eternally impact the lives of millions of people — saving them, healing them, performing miracles, and delivering them from Satan's bondage.

The Holy Spirit has manifested Himself in ways we had only dreamed of in years past before our adventure in the former USSR began. For instance, in the years since we arrived in 1991, He has enabled us to reach millions of souls through a weekly television program; establish three churches in the capital cities of Latvia, Russia, and Ukraine; launch a Bible school to train leaders for a multitude of churches; and hold crusades and meetings in the various regions to build up and strengthen local works.

The key for me has been to learn to work with God's Word while simultaneously flowing with the Holy Spirit. It's a learning process that each of us must pursue in order to grow in God and fulfill His purpose for our lives. And we can trust the Holy Spirit in that process. He never leads us contrary to the Word of God; rather, He confirms and supports it. After all, He is the One who inspired its writing (*see* 2 Timothy 3:16)!

With the Bible in our hands and our hearts — and with an open spiritual ear to hear what the Holy Spirit is saying — we are equipped with what we need to *never* fail. No people and no generation have ever been so blessed as those of us who live in this glorious Church Age!

I'm happy that you have picked up this book today. I believe that reading it will be the start of a marvelous new adventure and spiritual journey for you.

The fulfillment of the God-conceived desires that you have dreamed of and that your heart has yearned for lies in front of you, hidden in the keys within these pages. Read this book with an open heart, and ask the Heavenly Father to reveal the ministry of the Holy Spirit to you. As you act on what you learn and yield to His life-transforming work in your own life, you will set yourself squarely on the path that leads to your dreams becoming reality!

— *Rick Renner*

CHAPTER ONE

THE DEEPER DIMENSION

*M*any years ago when I was a young teenager, my heart began to search for a deeper walk with Christ. I had been raised in a denominational church and saved at an early age. Living the Christian life was not new to me or to my family. But more and more I began thinking, *Surely there must be more to the Christian life than what I'm experiencing!* It was as if there were a hole in the pit of my stomach, and I yearned for God to fill it up with Himself. I searched here and there, looking for someone who could help me find this deeper place in God that my heart longed for.

A key moment in this journey of mine occurred in 1973 when I walked into my aunt's home and heard a preacher on a teaching tape she was playing as he spoke about the ministry of the Holy Spirit. I had already begun searching before that day, but in the days and weeks that followed, I started asking more questions about the infilling of the Holy Spirit. I was getting hungrier and hungrier.

Then in January 1974, I was introduced to the power of God in a marvelous way the day I was baptized in the Holy Spirit. It was truly a glorious experience. Yet even after that landmark moment, I knew in my heart that there had to be something more than what I had already discovered about the Holy Spirit and a deeper dimension in my walk with God.

It would be months later in this search for more of God, as I flipped from one radio station to the next, that I would come across a most unusual program that absolutely captivated my attention. Over those radio waves, I heard the woman named Kathryn Kuhlman speaking about miracles and a relationship with the Holy Spirit. She had my attention.

I had heard of Kathryn earlier as part of this ongoing search. But that day as I sat in the kitchen near our radio, my ears were tuned to every word as she described a continually growing, intimate relationship with the Holy Spirit. My heart nearly beat out of my chest! I was so excited to hear someone speak about that deeper place in God that I so desperately longed for.

In the weeks that followed, I tuned in to Kathryn Kuhlman's radio program every day. She spoke so naturally about the Holy Spirit and her relationship with Him. She spoke of Him as though He were a real Person — an intimate Friend with whom she shared her mornings, her afternoons, and her evenings. She testified of miracles that occurred in services she held all over the United States. And every Friday, actual excerpts of those miracle services were broadcast on her radio program.

SPIRITUAL HUNGER
AND ENCOUNTERS WITH GOD

Everyone destined to grow in God eventually comes to a place of dissatisfaction in his or her spiritual life. This is the point where a new level of intimacy with God can begin. As Jesus said, "Blessed are they which do hunger and thirst after righteousness: for they shall be filled" (Matthew 5:6). Such people are blessed because their spiritual hunger and thirst starts them down a path that leads to a new encounter with God — and as they yield to that encounter, He *fills* them.

However, the season of spiritual hunger and thirst that precedes this infilling can be one of the most uncomfortable, unsatisfying periods a person can ever experience. Amazingly, it is this state of spiritual misery that drives a person to a position where God can reveal Himself to him or her in a more meaningful, personal, and powerful way.

> **Everyone destined to grow in God eventually comes to a place of dissatisfaction in his or her spiritual life. This is the point where a new level of intimacy with God can begin.**

Doctrinally and intellectually, I understood a lot about the work of the Holy Spirit at this time in my life. In our church, we were taught the truth about Him working to produce the character of God and the fruit of the Spirit in us, conforming us to the image of Jesus Christ. That teaching was superb, but it was primarily taught and received in the mental realm. It never put me in touch with the Holy Spirit's power in a real way.

But as I listened to Kathryn Kuhlman's radio program, I knew that this woman had a relationship with the Holy Spirit I had never experienced. I was completely mesmerized by what I was hearing from Ms. Kuhlman. I had never heard anyone speak to the Holy Spirit the way she did. I regularly talked to Jesus and my Heavenly Father, fellowshipping with each of them from my heart. But now this new thought struck my heart with the force of lightning: *Was I supposed to relate to the Third Person of the Trinity the same way this woman of God did?*

My heart was captured by what I was hearing about actually experiencing a relationship with the Holy Spirit. I wanted to experience the intimacy with Him that Kathryn Kulhman obviously knew and lived.

THE HUMAN HEART'S DEEPEST DESIRE

Most believers long to know a deeper place in God. There are multitudes of Christians who really love God but have no joy because they haven't experienced this deeper place in Him. Striving to please God and to do what is right, they go to church week after week, wondering why they feel so powerless and empty as Christians. But they faithfully keep up the pace, hoping that somehow, someday, it will all begin to "click" for them.

Meanwhile, these Christians feel guilty about the way they feel and dare not share it with anyone else. They keep their frustrations to themselves and hang on to the hope that maybe one day, it will all begin to make sense.

> There's nothing more miserable and defeating than to be a Christian, sincerely trying to live the Christian life, without really knowing the joy and power of the Holy Spirit.

If you've ever been in this condition, you know there's nothing more miserable and defeating than to be a Christian, sincerely trying to live the Christian life, without really knowing the joy and power of the Holy Spirit. That's why I have written this book. It is not meant to be a deep, scholarly work. Rather, it is a book designed to lead spiritually hungry people like you into a new place in God, a secret place that He has been waiting for you to find for a long, long time. It's the same place in Him that the early believers discovered — and it was the reason they could experience deep joy, even in the midst of terribly dark hours of persecution.

But now God is calling us onward to develop a practical working relationship with the Holy Spirit. Every one of us eventually reaches this turning point — a time when the heart is no longer satisfied and seeks for more. It is then that God's Spirit beckons us to draw closer, to enter a deeper place of intimacy with Him.

In the chapters to come, you will see that during the days of Jesus' humanity on earth, He lived in constant communion with the Holy Spirit. Jesus knew the intimacy, partnership, and responsibility of the Holy Spirit, not merely as a theoretical doctrine, but as a constant, daily reality. His relationship with the Holy Spirit was His source of power, His vehicle of divine revelation, and His strength to cope with the throngs of people who came to be ministered to by Him.

If the cry of your heart is to walk as Jesus walked and to know the power of the Holy Spirit as the disciples did in the book of Acts, you have picked up the right book. Now read on and see how you, too, can come to know personally the *intimacy, partnership*, and *responsibility* of the Holy Spirit.

A whole new realm in God awaits you!

Think About It

Whose voice on the earth is the most familiar to you? How would you describe the journey that led to that human voice becoming so familiar? The Holy Spirit wants you to get to know *His* voice better than you know any human voice. And He always has a new spiritual level, or realm, He is calling you to reach for and press into as you grow in your walk with God. For the hungry heart, there is never a place in Him that is "far enough."

As you ponder the unique pattern of the Holy Spirit's ways with you, can you identify what helps you actively keep pressing deeper and further in your relationship with Him? Where are you presently in your journey toward reaching the goal of developing a working relationship with the Holy Spirit? What are some of the distractions that can bump you off course in that pursuit if you're not careful to deal with them correctly?

CHAPTER TWO

THE DYNAMIC DUO

I will never forget that day when I was switching back and forth from one radio channel to the next, hoping to find someone who could answer my questions, and I suddenly heard beautiful piano music over the airwaves. The piano music drew me in, and I stopped at the channel to listen.

The announcer came on and said, "And here she is, that young lady you've been waiting for — Kathryn Kuhlman!"

Then I heard Kathryn's first words: "Hello, there! And have you been waiting for me?" Although this was her usual way of addressing her listeners every day, it seemed as if this woman were speaking to me personally.

She continued, "Today I want to speak to you about the communion of the Holy Spirit."

As I sat and listened to Kathryn's teaching, I realized that at last I had found the person I'd been looking for to help take me into a deeper walk with the Spirit of God.

I was captivated by this woman's teaching and the way she talked about the Holy Spirit. And when she announced she would be having a miracle service in Tulsa, I knew I had to be there. A new hope stirred in my heart.

'Please Don't Let Them Be Disappointed'

The meeting was to be held at the Mabee Center auditorium on the campus of Oral Roberts University. That Sunday I excused myself from our church's Sunday school a little early and drove across Tulsa to ORU to get ready for that afternoon's miracle service.

When I arrived, I couldn't believe my eyes! People were standing all around the massive Mabee Center. The streets and parking lots were jammed with buses and carloads of people who had driven hundreds, even thousands, of miles to get to this service.

I had never seen anything like it. I was grateful that my aunt had coaxed me into singing in the Kathryn Kuhlman choir, because choir members were taken right into the auditorium through a back-door entrance so we could begin rehearsing for the service. As I made my way in, I wondered, *Why have all these people come from so far to hear this woman preach?* It wouldn't be long before I understood.

The entire back half of the auditorium's bottom floor had been partitioned off for the critically and terminally ill. A huge crowd was standing outside, but the ushers were allowing those who were debilitated to come into that special area so they wouldn't have to fight through the crowds.

From where I sat, I could see wheelchairs, oxygen tanks, IVs, crutches, scores of people lying on stretchers, as well as doctors and nurses sitting in attendance to those who were infirm. It looked as if an entire hospital ward had been emptied and brought to the service! Some of the critically ill had been transported by family members. Others were so close to death that they had been brought to the meeting by ambulances.

One hour before the service began, the main doors to the auditorium were opened. The crowd rushed in as fast as their feet would carry them. It looked as if a sea of humanity had been released inside all at once! People scrambled here and there, each trying to get a good seat as close to the front as possible.

Soon the auditorium was filled, so the people who remained outside were diverted to an overflow room where they could watch the service by closed-circuit television. An air of excitement and faith flooded the auditorium.

I couldn't help looking back at the section reserved for the wheelchairs and stretchers. The people in that section were so sick. I knew that many of them had come to the meeting out of desperation. This was their last hope. I found myself praying quietly, "Oh, Lord, please don't let them be disappointed today."

The ushers walked up and down the aisles offering little booklets that contained testimonies of those who had received medically confirmed miracles in other miracle services with Kathryn Kuhlman. I reached out and chose three of the booklets and read them as I waited for the choir director to come onstage.

What amazing testimonies they were! By the time I had finished reading that third little booklet, I could sense my faith rising to a place it had never been before.

MIRACLES REALLY DO HAPPEN!

Moments before the service began, a crusade spokesman came to the microphone and announced that miracles had already occurred even while people were just sitting there, waiting for the service to commence. Once again I could sense my faith and the corporate faith of that massive congregation rise even higher. The expectation in that place was so strong, it seemed as if it could have lifted the building right off its foundation!

Then the choir director appeared before us, urging us to stand to our feet and get ready to sing. The huge throng of people stood with us as we sang and worshiped the Lord. Thousands of voices — Southern Baptists, Methodists, Catholics, Episcopalians, Presbyterians, Lutherans, Greek Orthodox, Pentecostals, and Charismatics — were all joining together in adoration and worship.

The entire crowd began to sing the words to the song "How Great Thou Art." As we did, Kathryn Kuhlman came out on the platform to sing with us. It was my first time to see her. Dressed in a long, white gown, she moved gracefully back and forth on the stage. In her deep contralto voice, she sang out, "Then sings my soul, my Savior God, to Thee; how great Thou art, how great Thou art!...."[1]

When the music and instruments stopped, Ms. Kuhlman welcomed the people and then led us as we all sang, "Alleluia." I remember thinking, *This must be what Heaven will be like.*

After some more music, Kathryn Kuhlman approached the podium and said, "I'm just going to speak to you for a few minutes today."

One hour later Kathryn was still speaking, and the crowd was so engrossed in what she was saying that no one noticed how much time had passed. It was as though we had all been invited in to view publicly the private, dynamic, and intimate relationship between this woman and the Spirit of God.

---

[1] "How Great Thou Art" by Stuart K. Hine. Copyright © 1953. Renewed 1981 by Manna Music Inc., 35255 Brooten Rd., Pacific City, OR 97135. International copyright secured. All rights reserved. Used by permission.

Here was a human being engaging in intimate fellowship with the Holy Spirit right in front of us. Although I had grown up in church all my life and had been saved as a young child, I had never seen, experienced, or even heard about what I was witnessing that day.

The sermon was fine, but watching this woman relate with the Holy Spirit was more dramatic and impacting than any sermon that could have been preached. This was the most moving thing I had ever seen in my entire life. It was wonderful beyond words.

Interrupting her own sermon, Kathryn moved across the stage and pointed her finger out toward a section of seats at the top of the auditorium and said, "Someone right up there has just received a miracle. Stand up and claim your miracle!"

A whirlwind of power passed through the auditorium, and miracles of healing started taking place throughout the auditorium. Soon people were lining up near the stage to testify about what had happened to their bodies. Wheelchairs were emptied; paralyzed people got up from their stretchers and walked; blind eyes were opened; deaf ears heard; and the dumb were now speaking.

For about three hours, I watched in amazement as the supernatural power of God continued on full display. Everything I'd ever dreamed, everything I'd ever wanted to believe in, was happening right before my eyes.

A LOOK AT A LIVING RELATIONSHIP

My questions about God's miracle-working power utterly dissolved as I watched those wheelchairs being emptied and people who had been brought in on stretchers walking, even running, from one end of the stage to the other. Soon the entire front of the auditorium and the aisles on the bottom floor were jammed with people who had come forward to give their lives to Christ.

What a powerful meeting that was! Not only did I see multiple miracles of the human body, but I also saw miracles of salvation for the human spirit! All my Baptist teaching about miracles no longer occurring was stripped away by the end of that service. And no one could accuse Kathryn Kuhlman of taking glory for herself. No one received the glory that day except Jesus Christ.

But the thing that struck my heart more than anything else, even more than the healings and miracles, was the vibrant, intimate relationship between the Holy Spirit and a human being that I witnessed during those three hours. It was something I had only dreamed was possible. How remarkable it was to watch Kathryn flow in the gifts of the Spirit and respond to the Holy Spirit's gracious, gentle leading. Surely God had brought me to this place to see the kind of relationship He wanted *me* to have with the Holy Spirit.

> **The thing that struck my heart more than anything else, even more than the healings and miracles, was the vibrant, intimate relationship between the Holy Spirit and a human being that I witnessed during those three hours.**

When the service was over, I looked at my watch and was shocked to see how late it was. As I was driving home from the meeting that evening, one thing had become very clear to me: *This woman knew a place in God I didn't know.* It wasn't her sermon or her style that produced that power. That power was a byproduct — an overflow, or a spilling over — of her daily relationship with the Holy Spirit.

I began to reason, *If it is possible for Kathryn Kuhlman to know the Holy Spirit in this way, it must be possible for me, too, since God has declared that He is not a respecter of persons* (*see* Acts 10:34). That afternoon, my perspective of spiritual things changed and came into clearer focus.

From that moment on, my heart's passion was for the Holy Spirit and me to become intimate, cherished friends. My heart and soul longed to discover the secret place in God I had witnessed that Sunday afternoon on the campus of Oral Roberts University. *I wanted to know the real-life fellowship of the Holy Spirit.*

THINK ABOUT IT

The undeniable demonstration of God's miracle-working power obliterates doubts and questioning. But there is a spiritual law that must be activated for that power to be released to its full potential — and that is an ever-deepening, personal communion with the Holy Spirit.

What about you? Do you have a desire to draw closer to the Holy Spirit in intimate fellowship and communion? Miracles in themselves could eventually leave a person feeling hollow and empty. But the communion of the Holy Spirit produces deep fulfillment that lasts. Consider specific steps you can take, beginning today, to cultivate this deeper walk with the Spirit.

CHAPTER THREE

AN INTIMATE, PERSONAL RELATIONSHIP WITH THE HOLY SPIRIT

*W*hen referring to the Holy Spirit, Jesus always used a personal pronoun. He called the Holy Spirit "He," "Him," or "Himself." Never once did Jesus refer to the Holy Spirit as "it" or as "a feeling" (*see* John chapters 14-16). For instance, in John 14:26, Jesus said, "But the Comforter, which is the Holy Ghost, whom the Father will send in my name, *he* shall teach you all things."

Jesus referred to the Holy Spirit with a personal pronoun because He related to the Holy Spirit as a real Person rather than as an invisible, intangible, mysterious, unknown entity.

Why is this so important? Because it tells us that as the Third Person of the Godhead, the Holy Spirit possesses the attributes of personality, just as the Father and the Son do.

We are made in God's image and therefore share these attributes. This means we are able to relate to the Holy Spirit personally. If He were an "it," it would be difficult to develop a relationship with Him. But the Holy Spirit has come to dwell within us, and He shares the very traits of personality that we are already familiar with. And He is at work in us to help us understand Him, know

Him, relate to Him, cooperate with Him, and enjoy fellowship with Him.

What kinds of personality traits does the Holy Spirit possess? He has every trait *we* possess, yet without a sinful nature. The Holy Spirit experiences and gives joy (*see* Acts 8:8; Galatians 5:22) and love (*see* Romans 5:5; Galatians 5:22), and He experiences sorrow (*see* Ephesians 4:30). And in John 14, 15, and 16, we read about a myriad of things He does that any person might do, such as help, encourage, comfort, coach, etc. You will see more of these in the later chapters of this book.

No one ever born on this earth knew the Holy Spirit better than Jesus. After all, Jesus was:

- with the Holy Spirit at the creation of the universe.

- conceived by the Holy Spirit in the womb of the virgin Mary.

- baptized by the Holy Spirit at the Jordan River.

- empowered to minister by the Holy Spirit.

- crucified in the power of the Holy Spirit.

- raised from the dead by the power of the Holy Spirit.

Once Jesus was raised from the dead and had ascended on High, the first thing He did was pour out the promised Holy Spirit on the Church. Jesus knew the Holy Spirit inside and out, and He related to the Holy Spirit in a personal manner. It is imperative that we learn to do the same.

It is critical for us to understand that the Holy Spirit has the attributes of *personality*. These attributes are the basis for all aspects of fellowship and relationship that we will ever enjoy with Him.

The leadership of the Early Church was well acquainted with the personality of the Holy Spirit. When they needed to make a crucial decision regarding the Gentile converts, they said, "For it seemed good to the Holy Spirit, and to us, to lay upon you no greater burden than these necessary things" (Acts 15:28 *NKJV*).

Early believers knew the Holy Spirit so well that even if they didn't receive a specific word from Him, they were able to make necessary decisions because they personally knew what "seemed good" to the Holy Spirit. They knew what He liked, and they knew what He didn't like. They knew what "seemed good" to Him because they had more than an intellectual knowledge of Him. They shared a real communion with the Holy Spirit.

When you know certain people in your life well — your spouse, your children, your close friends — you don't always have to ask them what they think. Sometimes you already know! You can tell what they think simply by looking at them. You've walked with them in life long enough to learn their personality and their responses to different situations.

If I get upset, my wife knows it without my telling her because she knows me. If I get excited about something, I don't have to tell Denise because she knows me well enough to know when I am excited. She knows me because she has spent time with me, lived with me, talked with me, prayed with me. Denise knows me better than anyone else. Likewise, no one knows Denise like I do.

We recognize human relationships easily because we can see the people in our lives with our eyes and touch them with our hands. Naturally, these relationships seem more tangible to us than our relationship with the Holy Spirit because He is invisible to our natural eyes and impossible to touch with the hands.

Nevertheless, the Holy Spirit's invitation to us to become intimately acquainted with His personality assures us that it is a very real possibility. But it's up to us to accept that divine invitation, just as the early believers did, and then begin to pursue with all our hearts a new level of communion with the Spirit of God. We must make it our highest priority to know the Holy Spirit in the same deeply personal way that Jesus knew Him.

Developing the Divine Romance

To know the Holy Spirit more intimately, we cannot ignore what Jesus said in Matthew 6:6: "But thou, when thou prayest, enter into thy closet, and when thou hast shut thy door, pray to thy Father which is in secret; and thy Father which seeth in secret shall reward thee openly."

What did Jesus mean when He said to "enter into thy closet"? Was He actually telling us to get up every morning, open the closet door, shove all our shoes and clothes to the side, crawl inside that dark room, shut the door, and pray? No, not at all.

The word "closet" is taken from the Greek word *tameion*, an old word that was first used to describe *a secret place where one would hide his or her most valuable possessions*. What would you do with a room like that? You'd keep it under lock and key. You wouldn't leave a room like that open where anyone could come in and traffic through your most precious possessions.

As time progressed, the word *tameion* came to mean *a safe place to put one's money or treasure*. In our modern context, the word could describe something like a safety deposit box at the bank.

But by the time of the New Testament, the word evolved to hold an even deeper meaning. The word *tameion* was used to describe *a bedroom*. A bedroom is a secluded place where the exchange of a treasured relationship transpires between a husband

and wife. Behind closed doors, their most intimate moments are shared only with each other.

You could actually translate this verse to say, *"When thou prayest, enter into thy bedchamber."*

Jesus used the word *tameion* to convey the idea of intimacy with the Holy Spirit. Symbolically Jesus was saying, *"Just as a husband and wife enter into their bedroom and shut the door so they can bare their hearts and souls to each other in intimacy, so also you should have a relationship with the Holy Spirit that is so tender, special, and intimate that it is shared only between you and Him — and no one else."*

This, of course, doesn't literally mean you must pray in your bedroom. The concept of a bedroom is used only to convey the idea of a single, isolated, solitary place. Jesus was describing the proper *attitude* and *environment* for prayer.

When we enter into prayer, it should be done at a place and time when we are not interrupted so the Holy Spirit can speak to our hearts and we can bare our hearts to Him. It is to be a mingling together of human spirit with divine Spirit in sweet communion.

Our daily top priority should be to make sure we carve out time in our schedule to enjoy this special time of intimate fellowship with the Godhead through the Holy Spirit. It doesn't matter where we do this, but it should be private. During this special time each day, we must put everything else aside and concentrate only on Him. This is a sacred time.

The gospels record that Jesus often prayed early in the morning when the other disciples were sleeping, often up on a mountain or out in the wilderness (*see* Matthew 14:23; Luke 6:12). There was nothing holy about that time of day or those particular settings. But in those early morning hours, Jesus found solitude and quietness with God, and on a mountainside or in the wilderness, He could pray without interference or interruption from others.

Your quiet place may be in your car when you are driving to work alone every morning. It may be early in the morning when everyone else in the house is still sleeping. Perhaps it is late at night after others have gone to bed. The point is that you must have a quiet place and time when you can give yourself wholly to the fellowship of the Holy Spirit.

A Matter of Choice

You might say, "Yes, I know I need to spend quality time with the Lord. But my schedule is so busy, it's difficult for me to find a time to do it." But please be honest with yourself. You know in your heart that you will make time for what is important to you.

- Do you have time to surf the Internet?

- Do you have time to watch the news?

- Do you have time to go to the movies?

- Do you have time for other forms of recreation?

You will always make time for what is important to you. If you really wish to have an intimate, personal relationship with the Holy Spirit, you will make time for it. It must become a priority as a matter of choice.

My wife and I have traveled and taught the Bible together for years. When our children were very young, I always found it a challenge to find a quiet place to pray and study.

When we'd arrive at our hotel room, the children were always so eager to get out of the car that it seemed as if they turned the hotel room inside out within five minutes! They were typical energetic little boys who would grow tired of riding in a car for hours at a time. While we were putting the room back together on one side, they were taking it apart again on the other side!

Denise and I had a typical routine that we'd follow on these ministry trips with our little ones. After breakfast, it would be time to put them down for a nap. Denise and I would use that time for study and meditation in the Word of God. Afterward, we'd have a meeting with the pastor in the latter part of the morning, and then we'd go to lunch.

> If you really wish to have an intimate, personal relationship with the Holy Spirit, you will make time for it. It must become a priority as a matter of choice.

Soon after that, it would be time to put the children down for another nap. While they were sleeping, we'd study again and prepare for the evening service. By this time, we'd be so worn out from managing the ministry and family time with our children that we'd also try to get some rest ourselves.

After the meeting each night, we'd eat a late-night dinner and fall into bed, hoping the children would sleep through the night with no problems. After a long stretch of this routine while on the road, both Denise and I would become desperate for some *real* quiet time with the Lord.

We tried getting up early, but it had to be *very* early because young children tend to rise with the sun. We would take turns using the hotel bathroom as our prayer closet. At times we prayed so quietly to keep from waking the children that we wondered if God could even hear us! And when we prayed with authority against the attacks of Satan in our lives, our prayers were so soft and quiet that it seemed as if we were just whispering at the devil.

Finally, Denise and I made a difficult decision. We determined to make our communion with the Holy Spirit the chief priority in our lives, regardless of any external circumstances. It required us to make schedule changes in our preaching itinerary that were hard to bear financially. But by making these changes, we were ensuring that both of us would be able to have daily, quality time with the Lord. And in the years that followed, we saw great reward in every area of our lives and ministry because of our obedience to keep our priorities straight.

Much has transpired since those early days of itinerant ministry throughout the United States. Our family moved to the former Soviet Union right after the fall of the Iron Curtain, and an entirely new set of external circumstances began to vie for our attention and time.

Today our lives are more productive than ever with the global assignment God has placed on our lives. We're still moving *at the speed of light!* And now besides three wonderful sons, we are privileged to have three lovely Russian daughter-in-laws, plus grandchildren! So even after all these years, Denise and I still have to decide to set aside time to be with the Lord — *as a matter of choice* — or it simply wouldn't happen.

We generally make time to do what we want to do in life. In other words, if it's important to us, we'll find time for it.

Our relationship with the Holy Spirit is the most important relationship in this world. I have learned that if my relationship with Him is strong, it makes my relationship with my wife and children good and strong. On the other hand, if I don't spend time communing with the Holy Spirit, it affects all my other relationships. I have learned that apart from Him, I truly have nothing to offer.

I have also learned that when I am in close fellowship with the Holy Spirit, He compensates for weaknesses in my life. In the next chapter, we'll see how the Holy Spirit did this in the life of Jesus as well.

THINK ABOUT IT

You can know the Holy Spirit as well as you want to. It's your choice to accept His invitation and make the decision to put all else aside that would distract so you can enter into a daily time of communion with Him. As you assess your daily schedule, what adjustments can you make to carve out a specific time that is solely focused on cultivating a deeper level of intimacy with the Holy Spirit?

CHAPTER FOUR

THE SECRET
TO SUSTAINING STRENGTH

I have often wondered, "How did Jesus have the physical strength to minister to multitudes of people without physically collapsing from the stress and pressure of it all?" I believe the answer lies in the consistency of Jesus to draw away and start His mornings alone with the Father in prayer, where He could gain and sustain the physical and spiritual strength He needed to minister to the masses.

This kind of sustaining strength was also evident in the apostle Paul's life. He faced a continual onslaught of grueling ordeals, yet he never seemed to wane in strength as he faced each trial bravely and victoriously. What was the secret to this sustaining power?

Paul gives us the answer in Philippians 1:19. In response to all the problems that were facing him, he answered, "For I know that this shall turn to my salvation through your prayer, and *the supply of the Spirit of Jesus Christ.*"

The phrase "the supply of the Spirit of Jesus Christ" is one of the keys to Paul's unbroken strength. The word "supply" is taken from the Greek word *epichoregeo.* The first part of the word, *epi,* means "on behalf of," and the second part of the word, *choregeo,* is the Greek word for *a choir or a choral presentation*. It is where we get the word "choreography."

So *epichoregeo* is an old word that literally means *on behalf of the choir*. What an important word this is for us to understand!

Thousands of years ago in classical Greece, a huge choral and drama company practiced endlessly for a huge, important theatrical performance. After they put in a great amount of time, effort, energy, and practice, it was finally time for the show to go on the road. But there was one major problem — they ran out of money!

These people had given their lives to this production. They had committed all their resources to making sure the performance succeeded. But because they ran out of financing, it meant the show was over — *finished*! They were washed up before the show ever officially got started. From all appearances, it was the end of the road for them and their dream.

Have you ever felt that way? Have you ever given yourself to something so completely that you didn't feel you had any more to give? Have you ever committed yourself to so much, so deeply, that in the end you didn't feel you had enough human strength to carry out your commitment, even though your desire was to fulfill it?

We all come to a time in our spiritual lives when we seem to have no more to give. We begin to wane physically and mentally. Even people with good intentions and a strong desire eventually come to one of these dead ends in their lives.

That is what happened to the choir in this classical Greek account; they had come to this very place. No funds meant *no show*! It seemed that all of that energy, practice, and commitment had been expended in vain. From all natural appearances, it was the end of their dream. But in reality, this dead-end place in their lives was the beginning of a yet unwritten part of their story.

At that moment of despair, a wealthy man stepped into the situation. He had heard about their commitment. He had heard about how they had worked on this project for so long. And because this wealthy man was so impressed with their dedication, he stepped into the middle of their situation and made a huge financial contribution *on behalf of the choir.*

This contribution "supplied" all that the choir needed to get back in business again! In fact, the gift the man gave was so enormous that it was more than they needed or knew how to spend! This man's contribution was *excessively large, abundant, overflowing,* and *overwhelming.*

This is where we get the word "supply" in Philippians 1:19: "For I know that this shall turn to my salvation through your prayer, and the *supply* of the Spirit of Jesus Christ." In light of this, Philippians 1:19 could be taken to mean: *"I am certain that this situation will ultimately turn around and result in my deliverance. I'm sure of it — first, because you are praying for me; and second, because of the special contribution of the Spirit that Jesus Christ is donating for my present cause."*

This means when you've given your best effort and you don't feel like you have another ounce of energy left to give, you have a divine promise to claim. When it looks like your resources are drained and you're unable to take one more step unless someone steps in to help you, that is *exactly* the moment when Jesus Christ becomes your personal Benefactor! Like the wealthy man in the story I just shared, Jesus steps into your life at that moment to donate a *massive, overwhelming, generous* contribution of the Holy Spirit's grace and power for your cause!

TIME TO RECEIVE

We all have experienced those times when it seems like we've come to a dead end in some area of our lives. That, however, is usually the moment we have the opportunity to truly learn how to live.

When we have nothing left to give, Jesus Christ picks up where we leave off through the ministry and power of the Holy Spirit. As we look to Him in simple faith, He makes an overwhelming contribution of the Spirit on our behalf, paving the way to finish what He started in us. Philippians 1:6 says, "Being confident of this very thing, that he which hath begun a good work in you will perform it until the day of Jesus Christ." However, we can cut off that supernatural contribution by failing to regularly set aside quality time with the Lord so we can receive His divine infusion of power as a continual supply.

> **When we have nothing left to give, Jesus Christ picks up where we leave off through the ministry and power of the Holy Spirit.**

If you will commit to making time every day to fellowship with the Holy Spirit and allow Him to become your cherished Partner and Friend, He will fill you with the strength you need in every situation. This is why your daily time with the Lord is so vital. You must learn how to enjoy fellowship with the Holy Spirit so that His power is free to work in you and through you, sustaining you through the most difficult times.

I encourage you to reevaluate your relationship with the Holy Spirit. Is He an "it" to you — just some invisible, unknowable part of God? Do you relate to the Holy Spirit according to the way He makes you feel or how your physical senses are affected by

His presence? As long as your answer to either of these questions is *yes*, you'll find it difficult to enjoy His partnership in your life. But how you view the Holy Spirit can change; His attributes and personality are revealed in the Word.

In the following chapters, you'll learn more about how to develop your fellowship with the Holy Spirit so He can become your trusted Partner. When this basic truth is established in your life, you will experience supernatural living by the power of God!

THINK ABOUT IT

In those moments in life when it seems you have expended all your energy and resources to accomplish what is yours to do, it's helpful to assess your relationship with the Holy Spirit. He is assigned to your life as your continual Teacher, Helper, Strengthener, Standby, and Guide. So it's good to evaluate: Have you been open and available to the Holy Spirit to receive the fullness of His supply when you need it the most? Or have you been relying, to some extent at least, on your own natural strength, experience, and resources to get the job done?

How you recalibrate your priorities and your "way of doing things" is the key to ensuring that you're in position to receive His supernatural supply of wisdom, strength, and provision in every situation.

CHAPTER FIVE

JESUS MADE A PROMISE

*I*f anyone understood the partnership of the Holy Spirit, it was the Lord Jesus Christ. Jesus' earthly ministry was completely dependent on the Holy Spirit. From Jesus' birth, nothing He did and nothing that happened in line with divine purpose in His life occurred apart from the power of the Holy Spirit. Moreover, the first thing Jesus did when He sat down at the Father's right hand in Heaven was to send believers the gift of the Holy Spirit. The ministry of Jesus and the ministry of the Holy Spirit are inseparable.

Consider these important facts about Jesus and the Holy Spirit:

- Jesus was conceived by the Holy Spirit in the womb of the virgin Mary (*see* Matthew 1:18,20; Luke 1:35).

- Jesus' conception in Mary's womb was confirmed by Elizabeth, Mary's cousin, when Elizabeth was filled with the Holy Spirit (*see* Luke 1:41-45).

- Jesus' dedication as a Baby in the temple was accompanied by the supernatural manifestation of the Holy Spirit as Simeon, the priest, and Anna, the prophetess, prophesied over Him (*see* Luke 2:25-38).

- Jesus' arrival to Israel as the Messiah was announced by John the Baptist. Under the anointing of the Holy Spirit, John declared that Jesus was the One who would baptize in the Holy Spirit and with fire (*see* Matthew 3:11; Luke 3:16; John 1:33; Acts 11:16).

- Jesus spoke of the baptism in the Holy Spirit and commanded His disciples to stay in Jerusalem until they had received this special endowment of power (*see* Luke 24:49; Acts 1:4,5).

- Jesus was empowered by the Holy Spirit at the Jordan River when He was baptized in water by John the Baptist (*see* Matthew 3:16; Mark 1:10; Luke 3:22; John 1:32).

- Jesus was given the fullness of the Spirit without measure (*see* John 3:34).

- Jesus was led by the Holy Spirit (*see* Matthew 4:1; Mark 1:12; Luke 4:1).

- Jesus returned from the wilderness in the power of the Holy Spirit (*see* Luke 4:14).

- Jesus stated publicly that His ministry was a result of the power of the Holy Spirit (*see* Luke 4:18).

- Jesus warned about the danger of blaspheming the Holy Spirit (*see* Matthew 12:31,32; Mark 3:28,29; Luke 12:10).

- Jesus taught about the work and ministry of the Holy Spirit (*see* Matthew 10:20; Mark 13:11; Luke 11:13; 12:12; John 7:39; 14:16,17; 15:26; 16:7-15).

- Jesus proclaimed that we must be born again by the Holy Spirit (*see* John 3:5-8).

- The Lamb of God without spot or blemish, Jesus offered Himself upon the Cross through the power of the Holy Spirit (*see* Hebrews 9:14).

- Jesus was resurrected from the dead by the power of the Holy Spirit (*see* Romans 8:11).

- Jesus breathed the Holy Spirit into the disciples after His resurrection (*see* John 20:22).

- After Jesus was exalted to the right hand of God, He poured out the Holy Spirit upon the Church on the Day of Pentecost (*see* Acts 2:1-4,33).

- Jesus instructed the disciples through the ministry of the Holy Spirit (*see* Acts 1:2).

Jesus and the Holy Spirit were always together while Jesus was on the earth. If Jesus needed this kind of ongoing partnership with the Holy Spirit in order to accomplish His divine role in the earth, you must have this partnership as well. Jesus sent the Holy Spirit to give you everything you need to be a victorious, successful, faith-filled, overcoming child of God in this world. With the Holy Spirit at your side, you are equipped for every situation in life.

Because no one has ever known the Holy Spirit better than Jesus, we must look to see what Jesus had to say about the Holy Spirit's personality, power, gifts, and character. In John 14, 15, and 16, Jesus gave us important instructions about how to develop our own partnership with the Holy Spirit.

Jesus Made Us a Promise

Imagine how difficult it must have been for the disciples to find out that Jesus would be leaving them, especially after walking with Him for more than three years and seeing Him perform miracle after miracle. It was natural that they would feel sorrowful as Jesus announced that He would soon be returning to Heaven.

To the disciples, it must have seemed as if they were facing the end of their wonderful encounter with the Lord and with the power of God. Living and walking with Jesus was more than they had ever hoped for in this world. With Him at their side, their lives had been filled with adventure, excitement, joy, victory, power, healings, and miracles.

What would life be like without Jesus? Would it ever be the same? Was this the end of their dream?

Experiencing feelings of insecurity and uncertainty would have been a normal reaction for anyone in the disciples' position. They had grown dependent upon the physical, visible presence of Jesus, something we've never experienced and therefore cannot fully comprehend. After He left, they were probably tempted to feel spiritually abandoned.

In the midst of these fears, Jesus promised His disciples, "I will not leave you comfortless..." (John 14:18). The word "comfortless" is taken from the Greek word *orphanos*, which is where we get the word *orphan*. In New Testament times, the word *orphanos* described *children left without a father*, or it could have described *students abandoned by their teacher*. In both cases, it is the picture of younger, less educated, less knowledgeable people feeling deserted by those they trusted and looked to for guidance.

Jesus was a spiritual father to the disciples. He knew they were completely reliant upon Him. They could not make it on their own in the world without Him. This is why He promised them, "I will not leave you like orphans." Two verses earlier He had told them, "And I will pray the Father, and he shall give you another Comforter, that he may abide with you for ever" (John 14:16).

The word "pray" is the Greek word *erotao*, a legal word that is generally used in the gospels to describe Jesus' prayer life. This particular prayer word indicates that the sending of the Comforter was so crucial to the disciples' survival that Jesus was going to the Father *to present His case* for them, almost as if He were legally defending them and their rights. This case would be so concrete, clear, and unmistakable that the Father would respond to Jesus' strong request by sending the Comforter, or the Holy Spirit, to help all those who called upon the name of Jesus.

It is also important to notice that Jesus said, "And I will pray the Father, and *he shall give....*" The Holy Spirit was the Father's gift to the Church. Peter talked about "the gift of the Holy Spirit" in Acts 2:38 (*NKJV*). This was the Father's gift, free and without charge, to everyone who declares Jesus Christ to be the Lord of his or her life. Yet the Holy Spirit was given in response to *Jesus'* request for the disciples and for us.

Another Comforter

It was obvious to the disciples that this Comforter was not a normal person whom they would be able to see, hear, and touch with their hands. Can you imagine the questions that must have been swirling in their minds at that moment?

This is why Jesus was so careful to use key words when He spoke to them about the coming of the Holy Spirit. Especially notice that Jesus used the word "another" in this verse. He said, "And I will pray the Father, and he shall give you *another* Comforter."

This Greek word conveys a strong message about the Holy Spirit. The verse could be translated, *"I will pray to the Father, and He will send you Someone who is just like Me in every way. He will be identical to Me in the way I speak, the way I think, the way I operate, the way I see things, and the way I do things. He will be exactly like Me in every way. When He is present, it will be just as if I am present because we think, behave, and operate the same."*

Earlier in John 14, we see this same concept reflected in the relationship between the Son and the Father. Philip said to Jesus, "Shew us the Father, and it sufficeth us" (John 14:8). Jesus' response to Philip was key: "Have I been so long time with you, and yet hast thou not known me, Philip? He that hath seen me hath seen the Father; and how sayest thou then, Shew us the Father?" (John 14:9).

Jesus is the *exact* image of God the Father. Hebrews 1:3 (*AMPC*) declares, "He is the sole expression of the glory of God [the Light-being, the out-raying or radiance of the divine], and He is the perfect imprint and very image of [God's] nature...."

Jesus reflects the character of His Heavenly Father in every way. So if you saw Jesus when He walked this earth, you saw the Father. Jesus gave this testimony about Himself: "Verily, verily, I say unto you, the Son can do nothing of himself, but what he seeth the Father do: for what things soever he doeth, these also doeth the Son likewise. For the Father loveth the Son, and sheweth him all things that himself doeth..." (John 5:19,20).

This means Jesus did only what He saw His Heavenly Father do. Consequently, one of the best ways to discern God's will for certain situations is to look at how Jesus responded to similar situations.

People often ask, "How do I know if God wants to heal the sick today?" Look to Jesus for your answer, because He is the perfect imprint of the Father's nature and will. When Jesus healed someone, it was a demonstration of the Father's will to heal. He never would have acted on His own or out of character with the will of the Father.

When Jesus cast out demons and delivered the demon-oppressed, it was again a demonstration of the Father's will to set the captive free. Every demon-oppressed person who came to Jesus found freedom. And Jesus never would have acted on His own or done something contrary to the will of God.

Jesus' life, words, attitudes, and actions during His earthly walk were the absolute manifestation of God's will and nature. The Father and Son are in unity in nature, in character, in thought, and in action. That's why Jesus said, "He that hath seen me hath seen the Father" (John 14:9).

When Jesus was teaching the disciples about the Holy Spirit, He took this truth one step further and used the word *allos* to make this point. As we've seen, the word *allos* means *one of the very same kind.* Just as Jesus is the perfect imprint and very image of the Father's nature, the word *allos* tells us that the Holy Spirit perfectly represents the life and nature of Jesus Christ.

In Jesus' earthly ministry, He did only what He saw His Heavenly Father doing. In the same way, the Holy Spirit as Christ's representative on earth does only what He sees Jesus doing. The Holy Spirit will never act on His own or out of character with the will of Jesus Christ.

I've often heard Christians ask, "I wonder what it must have been like to walk with Jesus. Wouldn't it be wonderful to walk with Him, talk with Him, and hear His voice?" But they're missing the point of why Jesus sent the Holy Spirit in the first place. *His assignment is to be the Helper who brings us the life of Jesus Christ.* Jesus told Philip, "If you've seen Me, you've seen the Father." Along this same line, Jesus tells us, "I presented My case to the Father, and He gave you another Helper who is just like Me in every possible way. If you have Him, you have *Me*."

We received the indwelling presence of the Holy Spirit in the new birth. Now it's up to us to open our hearts to the Holy Spirit and permit Him to be our Helper and to bring Jesus' life to every area of our lives on an ongoing, daily basis.

In addition to the indwelling presence of the Holy Spirit, we see the demonstration of His infilling work in believers' lives in the book of Acts. It is evident that those early believers operated in great power as a result of being baptized in the Holy Spirit.

Jesus' physical absence didn't stop the Early Church from performing miracles, raising the dead, casting out demons, healing the sick, or bringing multitudes to a saving knowledge of Jesus Christ. In fact, the ministry of Jesus was multiplied through the Church because the Holy Spirit was with and in them and operating through them. The Holy Spirit perfectly represented Jesus to the Early Church in every way.

So don't look backward to what you missed because you didn't live 2,000 years ago when Jesus walked the earth. Start opening your heart to the work of the Holy Spirit right now. He wants to represent Jesus to you, to your church, to your family, and to your city — just as He did in the book of Acts.

The Holy Spirit and His mission have never changed. We are the ones who have changed. We have limited Him with our unbelief and lack of understanding.

Let today be the day you start allowing the Holy Spirit to do what He was sent to do: help you in every area of your life as He brings you the life of Jesus Christ in its fullest dimension.

Think About It

Some things in our past and present would probably look different if we had known the Holy Spirit more intimately and yielded to His leading more thoroughly through the years. We align ourselves to receive the Father's best plan for our lives when we learn to let the Holy Spirit guide us every step of the way without limiting Him with our preconceptions, wrong choices, and low-level preferences.

In what ways can you help your future look like the Father's plan for your life? What steps can you take to learn to yield more completely to His promptings in your spirit?

CHAPTER SIX

THE HOLY SPIRIT, OUR COMFORTER

*J*esus called the Holy Spirit *the Comforter* (*see* John 14:16). He also used this name in John 14:26, John 15:26, and John 16:7. It's significant that Jesus repeatedly called the Holy Spirit *the Comforter* four times in the short space of three chapters. It's very evident that this aspect of the Holy Spirit's ministry to us was very important to Jesus.

The word "comfort" can have many shades of meaning in our individual and vastly unique lives and seasons.

For example, if you're tired of working long and laborious hours, comfort for you may be the opportunity to relax for a while on your couch every evening after work.

If your heart is broken because of a soured relationship, comfort may mean talking to a friend who will listen to your hurts without passing judgment or giving you advice that you already know.

Perhaps you feel as if the pressures of life are piling on top of you and you don't know what to do or where to turn. Comfort may mean having a friend step into your situation to pray with you and help you think through your ordeal to determine the necessary steps God would have you take next in your life.

If someone you love has just died, comfort to you might be as simple as having someone hug you and perhaps stay with you through the most difficult time of adjustment.

The point is this: What "comfort" means to each of us often depends on what we are experiencing in life at a given moment. This makes it all the more important that we find out exactly what this word "comfort" actually means in Scripture. We must not make the mistake of interpreting what Jesus said about the Holy Spirit in light of our own human experience, which varies from person to person.

In John 14:16, the word "comforter" is taken from the Greek word *parakletos*. It was first used in a legal sense to denote *one who pleaded a case for someone else in a court of law*. It described *a helper or an assistant who was always ready and on standby to help, assist, and strengthen*.

Parakletos was also used from time to time to denote *a personal counselor or adviser*. This is the picture of a coach who instructs his students and apprentices in the affairs of education, business, or life. Just as a coach interacts with his pupils, a *parakletos* would draw close to those under his care to *encourage, exhort, urge, counsel*, and *teach* them how to do a better job.

The Amplified Bible may best translate the word "comforter" with its varied nuances of meaning. John 14:16 (*AMPC*) says, "And I will ask the Father, and He will give you another Comforter (Counselor, Helper, Intercessor, Advocate, Strengthener and Standby), that He may remain with you forever."

THE HOLY SPIRIT COMES ALONGSIDE US

Now that we've discussed the meaning of the Greek word *parakletos,* translated "Comforter," let's look at the parts that make up this compound word: *para* and *kaleo.*

The word *para* simply means *alongside.* It always carries the idea of *proximity* or *geographical location.* It specifically speaks of being *very close to* or *alongside* someone or something.

The use of the word *para* in this verse carries the idea of *coming as close as you can possibly get to someone.* You would never use this word to describe your proximity to a stranger. The word *para* would be used to describe your closest relationships.

For instance, my wife Denise is *para* me. She lives with me, talks with me, shops with me, travels with me, preaches and pastors our church with me, and prays with me. She is always *para* me. We are *side by side, close at hand,* and *alongside each other* all the time.

When people are close to one another in this way, they affect each other. They may even begin to take on some of that other person's attitudes, feelings, personality traits, habits, and gestures. After a while, they know each other so well that they almost don't have to ask the other person what he or she is thinking.

Now that we see what the word *para* means, let's look at how that applies to the first part of the Greek word *parakletos,* translated "Comforter," in John 14:16. The first thing this tells us about the Holy Spirit is that He is *close by* and *alongside* us at all times. There's nothing distant about His relationship with us, so we never have to beg or plead for Him to help us. The Holy Spirit is always with us, wherever we may be.

At the moment of salvation, the Holy Spirit comes to live in us (*see* Ephesians 1:13). Although He lives inside us, experientially the Holy Spirit comes *alongside* to assist us in the affairs of life and to bring the reality of Jesus Christ into every situation we encounter — *if* we'll believe and be open to it. Practically speaking, from the moment we are born again through the rest of our lives on this earth, the Holy Spirit is available for us to draw on His partnership every minute of the day.

THE HOLY SPIRIT HAS A SPECIFIC MISSION

The second part of the word "Comforter" is the word *kaleo*, which means *to beckon or to call*. For example, Paul used a form of this word in Romans 1:1 when he said he was "...*called* to be an apostle, separated unto the gospel of God."

This is not a picture of someone yelling or calling out for the sake of verbal communication. The *kaleo* kind of calling has *purpose*, *intent*, and *a sense of direction*.

> Practically speaking, from the moment we are born again through the rest of our lives on this earth, the Holy Spirit is available for us to draw on His partnership every minute of the day.

For instance, God calls us to fellowship with Him, and He calls unbelievers to repentance and salvation (Matthew 9:13). In addition, both Paul and Peter used the word *kaleo* to describe God's call to salvation and to ministry for themselves and others (*see* Romans 1:1, 8:30, 9:11,24; 1 Corinthians 1:9, 7:15; Ephesians 4:1,4; 1 Thessalonians 2:12; Hebrews 9:15; 1 Peter 1:15, 2:9).

Paul specifically used the word *kaleo* to describe his call to apostolic ministry (*see* 1 Corinthians 15:9; Galatians 1:15;

2 Timothy 2:9). When he heard Heaven's call, that divine calling gave him a sense of direction, purpose, and definition for his life.

Thus, we see that the word *kaleo* carries the idea of *a summoning forth* to do something very specific pertaining to *purpose* or *destiny*. For example, we are called to salvation. We are called to service in the local church. And we can even be called to the ministry. The call is always to something that points to *specific intent*.

The call of God concerning a person's specific course in life gives that individual insight into the divine purpose, plan, and design for his existence. It changes everything when a person knows in his heart that the Father has summoned him forth to carry out a specific assignment at His request.

Because *kaleo* is the second part of the Greek word translated "Comforter," we can also know that the Holy Spirit has not accidentally assumed His role in our lives. Just as God called Paul and Peter to be apostles — and just as each of us has been given a specific assignment — He has called the Holy Spirit to do something very specific in this world. This divine call has given the Holy Spirit purpose and direction. You might say it has given Him a *job description*.

Furthermore, the Holy Spirit must do His job faithfully, knowing that He will answer to the Father who has given Him this assignment. So what did the Father call the Holy Spirit to do? *The Spirit of God is called to be our Helper in this world.* This is the Holy Spirit's chief purpose and responsibility on this earth.

THREE FEATURES OF THE COMFORTER

This chapter has described three important truths that we can glean from the word "Comforter" (*parakletos*). We could summarize these truths as follows:

1. The Holy Spirit remains close by us.

Doctrinally we understand that the Holy Spirit indwells and seals every believer at the moment of salvation (*see* Ephesians 1:13). But when Jesus referred to the Holy Spirit as the "Comforter" in John 14:16, He wasn't speaking theologically. Jesus was referring to the practical relationship with the Holy Spirit that we can enjoy on a daily basis.

We don't need to plead and beg for the Holy Spirit to come near because He is always nearby. In fact, His place alongside us is so permanent that Jesus said He would abide with us *forever* (*see* John 14:16).

Ultimately, by learning to accept and participate in this wonderful fellowship with the Spirit of God, we will be continually impacted and transformed in a powerful way by His presence in our lives. We will start to take on and produce the fruit of the Holy Spirit in us.

2. The Holy Spirit has a calling.

Just as Paul and Peter were specifically called to be apostles in the Body of Christ, the Holy Spirit received a specific "calling" from God the Father to do a specific job in this world. The Spirit of God is specifically "called" (*kaleo*) to be "alongside" (*para*) each believer at all times.

- He is with you when you are in the lowest pits of despair, and He is with you when things are going well.

- He is with you when you go to bed at night, and He is with you when you get up in the morning.

- He is with you throughout your day.

- He is with you when you pray, and He is with you when you don't pray.

- He is with you when you behave maturely, and He is with you through your moments of immaturity.

- He is with you when you go to work, church, the grocery store, the beauty salon, the ball game, the movies, etc. — *wherever you go!*

Everywhere you go, the Holy Spirit goes too. If you are a child of God, He is with you at all times, through all circumstances. That is His calling!

3. The Holy Spirit has a job assignment.

The Holy Spirit's job is to help us! That help may include convicting us of sin, empowering us for the work of the ministry, imparting spiritual gifts, healing other people through us, and so on. But these operations of the Spirit in our lives, as wonderful as they are, represent pieces of a larger picture. The big picture is the Holy Spirit fulfilling His role as Helper to us. All the other functions mentioned are simply different manifestations of His help.

The Holy Spirit is responsible for carrying out His heavenly mission, not according to our human demands, desires, preferences, or needs, but according to the will of God — the One who called us and sent the Holy Spirit to us in the first place.

This means you and I can be assured that the Holy Spirit will *never* fail at His job as it pertains to our lives. Whatever form of help we need at any given moment, the Spirit of God is ever within us and alongside us to be the help we need, right at the time we need it!

Think About It

You have access to the endless wealth of the Holy Spirit for the need of the moment. There's so much more available to you than you have yet accessed, and all it takes for you to begin to receive the "more" is for you to say from your heart, "*Yes, Holy Spirit.*" Consider what the "help" of the Comforter might look like for you in a variety of situations or challenges. Ask the Lord what adjustments you need to make in the midst of those situations so you can receive what you need from the Holy Spirit more freely.

CHAPTER SEVEN

THE HEAVENLY COACH

I believe the best way to translate Jesus' prayer in John 14:16 is this: *"And I will pray the Father, and He will give you another COACH."*

Let me tell you why the word "coach" is my favorite translation of the word "Comforter."

Picture yourself as one of the disciples. You've just seen Jesus ascend back to Heaven, and you're standing there, looking up at the sky, thinking about what it was like to walk with Him on earth for the past three years. Jesus was your Leader, Teacher, Mentor, Revelator, Prophet, Miracle-Worker, Healer, Pastor, and Lord. You didn't do anything without Him, and He showed you how to do everything you did. He was the center of your life and the focal point of your attention.

Jesus was the One who sent you out to preach and instructed you in what material to preach. He gave you authority to cast out demons. He told you how to speak to demons — and when not to speak to demons. He taught you how to lay hands on the sick.

Jesus showed you how to deal with religious leaders and how to conduct yourself as a minister of the Gospel. He taught you how to hold crusades and build a ministry. He even taught you how to handle money in the ministry (*see* Matthew 10:5-14).

For three years, you carefully followed the Master's orders and dared not take a step without consulting Him first. In the truest meaning of the word, Jesus had been your Coach.

But after His ascension into Heaven, Jesus was suddenly gone.

- *Who would direct you now?*

- *Who would guide you now?*

- *Who would show you how to pray?*

- *Who would show you how to minister?*

- *Who would lead you as Jesus had led you?*

- *Who would coach you in your daily decisions?*

We are in the same situation regarding Jesus as the disciples were when He ascended into Heaven. We don't have Jesus here physically for us to turn to. We can't seek Him face to face for advice or counsel.

Of course, we have the benefit of the Word of God, which reveals Jesus' life and character, His ways and way of thinking, and His basic truths and commands. However, regarding the specific details of life, such as how to pray about a certain situation or what job to take, we can't arrange a meeting to discuss those issues with Him face to face. One reason we look forward to Heaven so expectantly is our desire to finally look into the eyes of our Savior. But, thank God, we can meet with Jesus anytime we want to in *this* life through the Holy Spirit in prayer!

NEWBORN BELIEVERS NEED ANSWERS

When we come to Christ as newborn babes, direct from a world of sin and spiritual death, we know very little — if anything at all — spiritually (*see* 1 Peter 2:2). Some of us were born into the Kingdom of God in such ignorance that we didn't even know we had previously been a part of Satan's kingdom! Regardless of how educated we are in natural and intellectual matters, we are immature spiritually when we first get born again. True spiritual maturity takes time to develop in our lives.

The Early Church was comprised of people who had been pagans. They, too, knew very little about the work of Christ and the things of the Spirit. Nevertheless, their ignorance didn't hinder them from finding their place in Christ and becoming faithful church members whom God could use. As a result, the Early Church quickly became a spiritual powerhouse in that dark period of human history.

The good news is that the Holy Spirit has come to teach us everything we need to know. An unlimited supply of wisdom and revelation is available regarding God's plan for our lives and how we fit into His greater plan for man — *if* we'll listen to the Holy Spirit, cooperate with Him, and allow Him to do what He was sent to do for us.

It doesn't really matter what you know or don't know when you receive Christ. You have just received a resident Partner in your heart who knows all the answers you need. The "Heavenly Coach" of your team has both the winning game plan and the supply of strength and courage you will require to achieve victory.

Now you must learn to cooperate with the Third Person of the Godhead. This cooperation is the beginning of the partnership with the Holy Spirit that I wrote about earlier. Unfortunately, many people who have known the Lord for years don't know this. They've had the indwelling presence of the Holy Spirit for a long time, but they haven't known how to develop this dynamic relationship in their lives.

God wants you to know the Holy Spirit in a personal way. He wants you to begin relying on that relationship the same way Jesus did when He walked the earth. If Jesus needed the Holy Spirit's partnership, you can rest assured that you most certainly need it as well. But how do you develop this relationship?

How *does* a human being relate to the Holy Spirit?

Remember, the Holy Spirit is like a coach to us. So what does a coach do? If the coach is a baseball coach, he teaches you how to run from base to base, how to use your glove to catch the ball, and how to swing the bat and make contact with the ball. Your coach says, "Hold the bat at the base with your hands wrapped around it like this, and as that ball approaches you, swing as hard as you can!"

If the coach is an acting coach, that person teaches you how to become an actor or be a better actor. He will coach you on how to become more convincing, more dramatic, and more comical. He even teaches you how to cry when tears are necessary for a certain scene.

If the coach is a vocal coach, that person will teach you how to sing — how to make each breath last longer, how to push from your diaphragm to make the sound stronger, how to sing on key, and how to sing in a way that really represents the emotional content of the music.

A coach teaches, advises, corrects, instructs, trains, tutors, guides, directs, and prepares you for your upcoming assignment. If you're new at what you're doing, the coaching may include a little coaxing as you develop your confidence. A coach will encourage you as he shows you what you did wrong the last time and then tells you how to do it right the next time: "Do it a little differently here; press a little further there; don't try so hard here; try harder there," and so on.

A coach isn't there to hit the ball for you, perform the scene for you, or sing that note for you. He's there to coach you so that *you* can hit the ball, perform the scene, or sing the note to the best of your ability.

Like a master craftsman teaching an apprentice a new skill, the Holy Spirit will direct and guide you. He'll show you what's needed. He'll open your eyes, impress your mind with supernatural direction, and lift you up when you've stumbled. He will develop you, foster your growth, cultivate your gifts, and teach you about the things of God and about life.

First John 2:27 says, "But the anointing which ye have received of him abideth in you, and ye need not that any man teach you: but as the same anointing teacheth you of all things." This verse is not encouraging us to reject the instruction of good leaders. But it *is* joyfully telling us that even though it's important to receive instruction from the leaders or pastors God places over us, first and foremost we have the Holy Spirit to teach us. We are never left in ignorance!

That is why Paul could leave the church in Thessalonica with his heart at rest after having been with the congregation for only three weeks of ministry. He knew the Holy Spirit would start teaching them where he left off and that they would continue to grow without him.

THE SPIRIT OF TRUTH

We must learn to continually keep our spiritual ear tuned to the Holy Spirit's counsel and follow Him implicitly, taking each of our cues from Him. He must become our Heavenly Coach, and we must learn to accept His leadership. This means that once we know we've heard the Holy Spirit's voice, we must be willing to yield and concede to His divine guidance with no objections.

You may be thinking, *But wait a minute! Following the direction of the Holy Spirit is brand new for me. This sounds a little scary to entrust myself completely to the leadership of the Holy Spirit. I can't even see Him, so it feels difficult to fully surrender myself to His leadership. What is my guarantee that the Holy Spirit will not misguide me or lead me astray?*

This is why Jesus called the Holy Spirit "the Spirit of truth" three times (*see* John 14:17; 15:26; 16:13). In other words, He was saying, "You can trust the leadership of the Holy Spirit! He hasn't been sent to lead you down the wrong path, to cause you to make a wrong decision, or to give you guidance that is devilish and evil. He is holy. And He is the Spirit of *truth*."

> **Once we know we've heard the Holy Spirit's voice, we must be willing to yield and concede to His divine guidance with no objections.**

You can be sure that when the Holy Spirit puts a thought in your mind to do something, it is a right thought. When He plants an idea in your heart, it is a right idea. When He nudges you in your spirit to do this or that, He always has a right reason for it. He sees and knows something you don't know and is trying to guide and direct you according to wisdom. He is always the Spirit of truth, and as the Spirit of truth, you can bank on the fact that He will never mislead you.

Think about what Jesus taught in His very last message to His disciples before dying on the Cross. For three entire chapters — John 14, 15, and 16 — Jesus taught about the Holy Spirit in order to alleviate the disciples' fears about trusting Him. Jesus considered their relationship with the Holy Spirit important enough to devote His very last time of fellowship with them speaking at length about that subject.

The bottom line is this: If we are going to move beyond our fear of the unknown and experience real, supernatural Christian living, we must come to a place of surrender to the Holy Spirit. In this act of surrender, we give Him permission to be our Heavenly Coach.

The truth is, the Holy Spirit is always trying to coach and direct us, even when we aren't listening. He is always at our side. He is always speaking to us, directing us, encouraging us, and trying to help us make the correct decisions and choices in life. Whether or not we listen to Him, He is there because that is the job assignment He has received from God the Father. Whether or not we benefit from this Heavenly Coach depends on us. We have to *choose* to listen to Him and follow His counsel.

A baseball coach can't help an athlete unless the athlete chooses to follow his instructions. An acting coach can talk until he's blue in the face, but it won't accomplish anything unless the actor is willing to listen to and carry out the coach's directions. A vocal coach can see potential in a person's voice and try to instruct that vocalist in ways that will cause him to sing better. However, if the student refuses to listen and chooses to sing as he desires, the coach won't be able to produce the best results.

Likewise, we must give the Holy Spirit ultimate authority in our lives, learn to trust His leadership, and do what He instructs us to do. He is the Comforter sent by God to help make the fullness of Jesus' life a reality in our everyday experience.

However, if the Holy Spirit's divine assistance in our lives is going to be effective, He requires our ears, our hearts, our trust, and our obedience. Anything short of this will produce inferior results far short of the supernatural life we really desire. He is there to help us, but we must *let* Him help us.

Inadequacy Qualifies You for the Spirit's Help

Let's talk about telling unbelievers about Jesus. Most believers are terrified to witness. The very thought of sharing Christ with someone makes them inwardly tremble. Often they are afraid that they will say something wrong or that they won't know how to answer a question.

The Holy Spirit was sent to witness about Jesus, which means He knows how to do that job (*see* John 15:26; Acts 1:8). If we will allow the Holy Spirit to lead us, He will show us how to witness to our friends and neighbors. He *knows* how to witness!

Praying for the sick is another difficult task for most believers. Many know very little about healing, which often becomes their excuse to explain why they never to do anything about it. "I can't pray for the sick because I don't know how." When their pastor exhorts them to get more involved in ministry to the sick, they think, *What do you mean, Pastor? I thought YOU were supposed to do that kind of thing. I didn't know when I came to this church that you were going to ask me to help pray for the sick. I don't know how! I feel totally inadequate.*

But the Holy Spirit knows how. He knows exactly why people are sick and why they are not getting healed. He knows if bitterness or unforgiveness is in their hearts, hindering them from being healed. He sees and knows it all. Therefore, He simply needs a willing vessel through whom He can deliver His healing power. The Holy Spirit knows how to heal the sick!

Inadequacy is not an excuse in the Kingdom of God. Inadequacy simply qualifies you for the help of the Holy Spirit. The sooner you realize your weaknesses and inadequacies, the sooner you'll be released into the supernatural help the Holy Spirit wants to give you. That recognition leads to the next revelation: The Holy Spirit must become your Strengthener and Guide.

It doesn't matter whether or not you are trained. You have a Heavenly Coach in your life who knows how to witness and how to heal. If you will listen to Him, read His Word, and allow Him to have His rightful place in your life, you will discover Him to be a Partner who is right at your side, showing you how to witness and how to pray for the sick.

> Inadequacy is not an excuse in the Kingdom of God. Inadequacy simply qualifies you for the help of the Holy Spirit.

As I was growing up in my denominational church, before I was baptized in the Holy Spirit, I didn't know how to witness. I was terrified at the thought of it. "What do you mean, knock on doors? Oh my, what am I going to say if someone answers the door!"

According to Acts 1:8, I knew the Holy Spirit was supposed to give us power to be witnesses, but I had rarely, if ever, personally experienced that power whenever I tried to witness for Christ. Each week I'd go from door to door with great inner frustration, always breathing a huge sigh of relief when our duty was done until the next week.

In our church, it was our desire to be the best witnesses in the whole world. The problem was that we wanted the power to witness, but we didn't want the Holy Spirit giving us an Acts 2:1-4 experience! In essence, we were saying, "Yes, we want the Holy Spirit's power, but on *our* terms."

As Christians, we should train, study, and prepare as much as we can to educate ourselves better for witnessing. But it's all in vain unless the Holy Spirit is working alongside us. Jesus told us, "Ye shall receive power, *after* that the Holy Ghost is come upon you: and ye shall be witnesses unto me..." (Acts 1:8). In John 15:26, Jesus also said, "...The Spirit of truth, which proceedeth from the Father, he shall testify of me."

In fact, the Holy Spirit's favorite subject to talk about and testify of is Jesus Christ. Witnessing from the heart comes naturally for the Holy Spirit. Since it's so natural and easy for the Holy Spirit, why has it seemed so hard, laborious, and joyless at times when we've done it?

The obvious answer is that we're doing it without the partnership of the Holy Spirit. When He is able to work through yielded vessels — believers who have opened their hearts to Him — He pours forth His joy, His excitement, His vitality, and His resurrection power upon the lost, and they are saved. If we are really listening to the Heavenly Coach, witnessing is easy!

> The Holy Spirit's favorite subject to talk about and testify of is Jesus Christ. Witnessing from the heart comes naturally for the Holy Spirit.

On the other hand, witnessing without acknowledging the Holy Spirit's help can amount to nothing more than an exercise in frustration. If we aren't yielded to Him so that He can supernaturally testify through us, we often turn to preplanned programs that can end up hindering the full release of the Spirit's power — and putting us in bondage as we witness.

However, I believe that those who are not filled with the Holy Spirit and don't intend to learn how to flow in His supernatural life probably *should* work with those preplanned programs. And the truth is, those programs can be helpful to those who witness about Jesus to others, including those who are Spirit-filled. They help form a structure in people's minds to help them get off the ground, so to speak, when they're witnessing.

Yet without the Holy Spirit's help, a person is left completely to his own abilities to do the job. And he will find that it's very difficult, if not impossible, for his mental abilities and talents to awaken the spiritually dead.

No wonder people feel so defeated when they witness without drawing on the leading and the power of the Holy Spirit. Thank God, there is a higher and a better way.

We find that higher way in the book of Acts. This account recorded the kind of testifying and witnessing that changed cities and shook nations! The early believers had no preplanned programs or witnessing courses, yet they changed history. Why? Because they had a vital relationship with the Holy Spirit, who is the greatest Witness and Testifier of Jesus on earth! Great success was the result.

The Holy Spirit still wants to tell the world about Jesus today. He still longs to release His power through the Church to turn the world upside down with the Gospel of Jesus Christ. That's the kind of power the Holy Spirit, our Coach, can release through *us* if we will take our cues from Him and do what He tells us to do!

Think About It

The Holy Spirit doesn't give us a stone when we ask for bread (*see* Luke 11:11-13). Whatever we need — comfort, wisdom, supernatural rest or strength, counsel, etc. — it is ours for the receiving at any given moment. Every day and in every situation, the Father expects us to trust Him for His supply through the Holy Spirit's ministry to us. We are to draw from the Holy Spirit's strength and wisdom, listen for His leading, and yield immediately to do what He prompts us to do.

Look for situations in your own life where a low-level way of thinking has dominated you and kept you separated from the reality of a vital partnership with Him. Do you need to step aside and spend time with the Holy Spirit to discover His "higher ways" of doing things in those situations?

CHAPTER EIGHT

BEING LED BY THE HOLY SPIRIT

*S*o often we just go with the "preplanned program" of the day and miss what the Holy Spirit is attempting to say and do through us. It seems we have become so programmed in every realm of life that it is amazing He is able to talk to us at all!

We have so many voices speaking to us through books, audio recordings, the Internet, public ministry, etc. With all of that filling our minds, we can be tempted to take all the information we've accumulated and run with it without consulting the Lord about it. That information, however, may not contain a single word that the Holy Spirit wants us to run with in our personal race!

Information is not the same as divine revelation.

The following statement may be difficult for us to accept, but it's true nonetheless: A great deal of what we have accomplished in life was actually initiated by us and not by the Holy

> So often we just go with the "preplanned program" of the day and miss what the Holy Spirit is attempting to say and do through us. It seems we have become so programmed in every realm of life that it is amazing He is able to talk to us at all!

Spirit. After we had already gotten the ball rolling on "our thing," we prayed and asked God to bless what we'd initiated, assuming that it was His will because it was a good idea. No wonder we had such poor results!

We must learn to put on the brakes, stop ourselves for a while, and wait before the Lord until the Holy Spirit speaks clearly to our hearts about the decisions we must make or the direction we must go. Although it may seem as if this way of doing things takes longer, the results will be more rewarding and long-lasting when He does speak and we obey. Furthermore, we will avoid pitfalls that could cost us a lot of time and effort in the long run.

Learn When To Wait

We must allow the Holy Spirit to lead us in every area of life. Take the subject of ministering healing as an example. Perhaps you have said at some time in your walk with God, "I'm going to pray for the next person in a wheelchair I meet, and that person won't need that wheelchair after I finish praying!" But when you finished praying, nothing changed in that person's condition. If you have gone through that kind of situation or a similar experience, you may have felt embarrassed, powerless, and defeated.

But wait a minute. Didn't God want to heal that person? Of course He did. But the anointing may not have been present at that exact moment to heal in that particular way. Or that person may not have been ready to receive with his or her own faith.

Being sensitive to the Holy Spirit will help you know when to pray and when to wait — and how to pray privately about a situation in the meantime *as* you wait.

A classic example of "waiting versus not waiting" can be found in the account of the two blind beggars in Matthew 9:27-31.

These two beggars heard Jesus walking by, but He didn't stop to heal them. The Scripture says that they "...followed him, crying, and saying, Thou son of David, have mercy on us."

The word "followed" is the Greek word *akoloutheo*, which means *to follow after someone or something in a very determined and purposeful manner*. Even though these beggars were blind and couldn't see where they were going, they were determined to follow Jesus until they got His attention.

Look at what these blind beggars did to get Jesus' attention. The verse says they were "crying" out. The word crying is the word *krazo*, and it means *to scream, yell, exclaim*, or *to cry out*. In other words, they were screaming at the top of their lungs to get Jesus' attention!

This is a very dramatic picture. Think about it. Here were two blind men, desperately wanting to be healed, who were screaming and yelling to get Jesus' attention. Yet He just continued walking as if they weren't even there.

Pursuing Jesus relentlessly, the beggars groped along in their darkness, still screaming, yelling, and crying out for Him to heal them. He couldn't have missed them because they were yelling so loudly. Yet Jesus didn't stop. Meanwhile, they were yelling at the top of their lungs, over and over again, "Have mercy on us! Have mercy on us! Have mercy on us! *Jesus, thou son of David, have mercy on us!*"

For years this passage of Scripture perplexed me. Why didn't Jesus acknowledge those two blind beggars? Why didn't He heal them? They were so determined to get His attention that they followed Him all the way to the house where He was staying, crying, "Son of David, have mercy on us!"

Finally, Jesus turned around and asked them, "Do you believe I can do this?" (v. 28).

They answered, "Yes, Lord."

Then Jesus touched the two beggars' eyes and said, "According to your faith be it unto you" (v. 29). Why didn't Jesus stop and heal them when He first saw them? Why didn't He immediately turn to heal them when He knew of their blind condition? And why did He answer them, "According to your faith be it unto you"?

Jesus evidently didn't sense the healing anointing at that moment; otherwise, He would have stopped to do it. However, this didn't hinder the beggars from receiving the healing that their hearts were crying out for. It was as though Jesus said, "I don't sense the anointing of the Holy Spirit to heal right now, so you're going to have to receive this one on your own faith! According to your faith, be it done unto you."

The only reason Jesus wouldn't have stopped to heal those two blind men is that the Holy Spirit wasn't leading Him to heal at that moment. The good news is that they could use their own faith to be healed anyway. They did — and they were healed!

When the Holy Spirit did lead Jesus to individuals who desired to be healed and made whole, Jesus healed them with a perfect, 100-percent success rate. We see this in Luke 6:19: "And the whole multitude sought to touch him: for there went virtue out of him and healed them *all*."

Another example is found in Luke 5:17, when Jesus was teaching the Word of God and He sensed that "...the power of the Lord was present to heal them." Following the leading of the Holy Spirit, He ministered to the multitude and healed a paralytic.

That was the key to Jesus' success in ministry: *He followed the leading of the Holy Spirit — every time.* We can do no less if we want to be Jesus' hand of love extended in the situations we encounter in life.

Learn To Follow the Leader

Luke 4:1 says that Jesus was "...led by the Spirit into the wilderness." Luke 4:14 says that He "...returned [from the wilderness] in the power of the Spirit...." Jesus was Spirit-led in everything He did. He relied totally on the Spirit to guide Him.

My two sisters and I used to play a game called "Follow the Leader" when I was a little boy. I always wanted to be the leader, but my older sister always ended up in that coveted leadership role.

> That was the key to Jesus' success in ministry: *He followed the leading of the Holy Spirit — every time.*

The leader told us what to do, what games we would play or not play, who would clean the house, and so on. Basically, we had to do whatever the leader told us to do. *No wonder my older sister always wanted to be the leader!*

I always think of this when I read Romans 8:14. It says, "For as many as are led by the Spirit of God, they are the sons of God." In Greek, the sentence structure is reversed so it reads, *"For as many as by the Spirit are being led, they are the sons of God."* It puts the Holy Spirit at the first of the verse, and we are placed behind Him — like the children who play Follow the Leader!

The Greek word for "led" is *ago*, which simply means *to lead.* But it must also be pointed out that this word forms the root for the Greek word *agon*, which describes *an intense conflict*, such as a struggle in a wrestling match or a struggle of the human will. This description stresses the fact that the Holy Spirit continually desires to lead us, but our human will does not *like* the idea of being led.

Thus, when we choose to walk in the Spirit and let Him dictate our lives, His leadership over us creates a struggle in our will — the choice between listening to our spirit man or yielding to our flesh. If we are more flesh-oriented, we are often afraid to trust the Holy Spirit. It is the nature of flesh to want to go its own way and distrust another's instruction.

When I was a child and we played Follow the Leader, I didn't like being led by my sister and being told what to do. I would rather have been in charge myself and called the shots as *I* saw them!

However, as children of God, we must learn to stay in our place with Him, which is never in the leader's role but *always* in the follower's role. We are not to be out front directing the Holy Spirit! It is always our place to position ourselves behind Him, following His lead, direction, and guidance. The mark of a mature believer is his or her ability to sense where the Lord is leading and then to follow that leading — even if that leading at the moment means to *stay put*!

Just knowing that the Greek word for "lead" is the root word for "struggle" arms us with wisdom for the coming battle! God is preparing us to deal with our flesh as we proceed into the Spirit-led life. The flesh wants control, so we must *mortify* (or defeat) the flesh and allow the Holy Spirit to have His way (*see* Romans 8:13; Colossians 3:5). Regardless of how great the struggle seems, this process of mortification and trusting the Holy Spirit's leadership is the *only* way to live a supernatural Christian life.

In a certain sense, we should make it our goal to be the Holy Spirit's continual "tagalongs." We should always be seeking to understand what the Holy Spirit is doing, where He is going, and how He is leading. Then once we know what He wants us to do, we are to follow His leading implicitly.

That's how Jesus related to His Father. Whatever Jesus saw the Father doing, that's what He did. In the same way, we must be sensitive to see what the Holy Spirit is doing and where He is leading and then follow His cues. That is being "led by the Spirit," which is both our responsibility *and* the benefit we enjoy as children of God. To become the mature Christians God wants us to be, we *must* have this practical, vital relationship with the Holy Spirit.

Often the way the Holy Spirit leads is by giving you an impression or a nudging in your heart to take a certain action. His leading can also be more dramatic, such as through prophecy or a vision — or simply as a "still, small voice" speaking to your inner being with a clarity that often enables you to actually quote what He said.

> **Whatever Jesus saw the Father doing, that's what He did. In the same way, we must be sensitive to see what the Holy Spirit is doing and where He is leading and then follow His cues.**

But regardless of the way the Holy Spirit chooses to guide you in a given situation, your pursuit of Him should always remain constant. As a child of God, learning to know His voice and to be led by Him should be one of your primary goals every day of your life as a child of God.

Think About It

Sometimes the most spiritual thing you can do about a situation is "nothing" — at least, nothing that is discernible on the outside. Sometimes that "nothing" is an act of wisdom as you wait before the Lord and actively seek Him for His leading, wisdom, etc.

Look at every area of your life and evaluate how closely you're following the leading of the Holy Spirit in each area. Think of instances in your life when you've jumped ahead and followed a plan of your own design. Compare the outcomes of those situations to what resulted from the times when you knew you'd received the guidance of the Holy Spirit and followed through on what He told you to do.

CHAPTER NINE

DAILY ADVENTURES WITH THE HOLY SPIRIT

The Holy Spirit sees what we cannot see and knows what we cannot naturally know, and He can be everywhere at all times. As human beings, we are limited in what we can see, hear, and know. Therefore, for us to minister successfully, we must listen to the Holy Spirit and allow Him to direct our thoughts, our words, and our actions.

Let me give you a simple example of the way the Holy Spirit coaches and leads us. One day Denise and I were shopping in a large grocery store. As we walked down the fruit aisle, my wife got a quizzical look on her face. "Rick," she said, "the Holy Spirit just put it in my heart to go witness to that woman over there. I believe He has given me something specific that I'm supposed to tell her."

"Then you had better obey the Lord," I told her.

"I'll be back in just a minute," she said.

Denise went over to the woman and said, "Ma'am, I realize you don't know me, but the Spirit of God told me to come over and tell you something. He said that you think God doesn't love you anymore and that He could never love you again. But He *does* love you and He wants you to know it."

This woman looked at Denise as though she were going to slap her right on the spot. Her facial expression said, "Get out of my way, you religious fanatic!"

After that reaction, Denise came back feeling like a total failure who had surely mistaken what she was supposed to do. "Rick, maybe I was wrong about the word I gave that woman," she told me. "She sure didn't seem too happy about hearing it."

"Sweetheart, turn around," I said. "That lady is walking toward you right now."

When Denise turned around, she saw the woman walking toward her with tears streaming down her face. The woman said, "I just went through a divorce, and someone told me that God would never love me again. I don't even know God! Can you pray with me to know Him?"

Right there in the fruit aisle of the grocery store, my wife led that dear lady to receive Jesus Christ as her Lord and Savior. Her salvation was the product of my wife's partnership with the Holy Spirit! He is the Heavenly Coach who is called alongside to help us in our testimony to the world.

THE COACH'S TIMING

I can see why the Holy Spirit is called the Comforter, because it's so comforting to know that He is always alongside us, especially when He asks us to do something that is different than what we're accustomed to doing.

For instance, what a revelation it was when I discovered the gifts of the Holy Spirit were not limited to church services! The gifts of the Spirit are to operate anywhere, just as they did in the book of Acts. The gift of miracles is supposed to be working through believers on the streets of our cities. Believers are to get people healed and set free, just as in Acts 3:1-8 when the crippled man was healed on the steps of the temple!

If we will listen to our Heavenly Coach, He will nudge us to witness when it is exactly the right moment. He'll put a word in our hearts, a "word of knowledge" (see 1 Corinthians 12:8), that will supernaturally speak to the heart of someone in need.

One day while I was eating in a restaurant, a waitress walked up to my table to take my order. The Holy Spirit prompted me in my spirit to minister to her, so when she left, I asked, "Lord, what do You want me to say to this woman when she comes back?" As I sat quietly, thoughts formed in my spirit. I began to understand what He wanted me to say to the waitress. In my spirit, I heard the Holy Spirit — my Partner and my Heavenly Coach — give me a very specific word of knowledge about this woman's situation in life. It was so specific, I thought, *This is either really right or really wrong!*

I heard the Holy Spirit tell me, *"This woman is a single mother who just moved here three weeks ago. She has three children, and she doesn't know how her bills are going to be paid. She is very worried, and I want you to tell her that I am with her in life, especially right now, and that everything is going to work out all right for her. She needs My peace to be ministered to her troubled mind, so speak to her now."*

When this woman returned to pour more coffee in my cup, I said, "Excuse me, may I have a word with you?"

She said, "Yes, what is it?"

I said, "As you turned away from me a few minutes ago, God spoke to my heart to tell you something. Three weeks ago you moved to this city with very little money. You have three children, and you don't know how you're going to pay your bills. You're feeling like you're all alone in the world, but, as you can see, God is working in your life. He is with you, especially right now, and He said everything is going to work out all right for you. He knows you so well that He has told me to speak this specifically to you today so you'll be aware of the fact that He's with you. So be at peace — You're not alone!"

Tears began streaming down that waitress's face. Every word had been correct. The Spirit of God had met her need because He had a vessel through whom He could speak. That day the partnership of the Holy Spirit helped a hurting woman experience the life of Jesus Christ. (And you can bet that I left a substantial tip for this waitress that day! God was making it very clear how much He loved her.)

WE MUST YIELD AND COOPERATE

If we will listen, the Holy Spirit will also speak to us in ways that seem less spectacular but are still life-changing. For example, He'll tell us when to be quiet at home and stop nagging our spouses! He will tell us to be more encouraging. He will exhort us to love our spouses in more expressive ways. He will show us how to be better parents and grandparents. He will show us how to be faithful in paying our bills.

If you're thinking, *I've never experienced anything like that before*, your problem may be that you're not listening to the Holy Spirit. He's probably talking to you all the time, trying to nudge you to do certain things. Perhaps you've been ignorant of who has been speaking to you, or perhaps you weren't listening. He's probably constantly planting thoughts and ideas in your heart, but you're not aware it is the Holy Spirit trying to guide and direct you.

The Holy Spirit will conform you to the image of Jesus Christ as you read His Word and seek to develop His divine partnership in your life. He already indwells you. Now you must learn how to enjoy Him and cooperate with Him in your practical, everyday life. He wants to use you to minister to others and to speak to you about your life.

But remember — a coach can do no good unless you listen to him!

Human beings are generally afraid of the unknown. As we already saw, it was for this cause Jesus told us three times that the Comforter was the "Spirit of truth" (*see* John 14:17; 15:26; 16:13).

The Lord knew we could be frightened about following someone we cannot see. After all, if we make a fool of ourselves, we can't say, "It's His fault," and point to someone standing next to us whom no one else can see! Besides having that hurdle to overcome, we also have to deal with the natural fear that we might go off the deep end and become wild, religious fanatics who live in an imaginary world.

But the Holy Spirit is "the Spirit of truth" — *not* the spirit of error or deception! He isn't going to misguide you. Nor will He lead you into something that is wrong and destructive to your testimony as a sound Christian thinker and believer. You can maintain a sound mind and be supernaturally led at the same time.

If the Holy Spirit drops a thought into your mind to do something, there is a reason He wants you to do it. If He tells you something will work, it will work. If He gives you instruction, His aim is to help you. He was not sent to hurt you or to make a fool of you. He was sent to make you better and more productive — a powerful, stable witness for Jesus Christ.

> If the Holy Spirit drops a thought into your mind to do something, there is a reason He wants you to do it.
> If He tells you something will work, it will work.

As you read this, you may be saying in your heart, *I want to know the Holy Spirit in this way. I truly do desire to conquer my fears and inward struggles and to let Him become my Leader.* If so, I encourage you to pray this prayer:

"Holy Spirit, I want to learn to trust You more. I want to discern Your leadership in my life and allow You to lead, guide, and direct me. This is new for me, so please keep speaking, instructing, prompting, and nudging me until I break free from my fears and learn to trust You."

THINK ABOUT IT

In a very real sense, the Holy Spirit acts as the divine Potter, shaping and molding us until we conform to the image of Jesus by the will and desire of the Father. But for that process to be fully effective, we first have to trust the Potter's hands on our lives. Our trust is the prerequisite to our yielding to His shaping and molding work, even when it's uncomfortable and unfamiliar. Because we trust Him, we can rest, knowing that He is at work only for our good and for the fulfillment of our God-ordained purpose on the earth.

Do you trust the Holy Spirit enough to yield to the process of change He must work in you, no matter how uncomfortable that process may be at times?

CHAPTER TEN

THE HOLY SPIRIT COMFORTS AND INDWELLS

*I*n the next few chapters, we're going to consider ten aspects of the Holy Spirit's work in our lives that He does for us on a *personal* level. They can be summarized as follows:

1. The Holy Spirit comforts us (John 14:16).

2. The Holy Spirit indwells us (John 14:17).

3. The Holy Spirit teaches us (John 14:26).

4. The Holy Spirit reminds us (John 14:26).

5. The Holy Spirit testifies with us (John 15:26).

6. The Holy Spirit convicts us (John 16:9).

7. The Holy Spirit convinces us (John 16:10).

8. The Holy Spirit guides us (John 16:13).

9. The Holy Spirit reveals to us (John 16:13)

10. The Holy Spirit helps us worship (John 16:14).

The first two responsibilities listed represent *the work the Holy Spirit does in our hearts.* We will begin by reviewing what Jesus taught about the Holy Spirit as Comforter.

1. The Holy Spirit Comforts Us

And I will pray the Father, and he shall give you another Comforter, that he may abide with you forever.

— John 14:16

Jesus used the name "Comforter" four times to describe the Holy Spirit — more than any other name given to the Spirit of God. When a truth is repeated over and over again in Scripture, it is done for the sake of emphasis.

The word "Comforter" comes from the word *parakletos,* which describes *one who comes to help, assist, exhort, encourage, counsel, advise, and strengthen.* It also portrays the idea of *a friend who steps into a difficult situation to defend you from something bad or hurtful.*

Jesus taught so extensively about the Holy Spirit because He wanted to alleviate any fears or misgivings the disciples may have had about the Holy Spirit, whom they could not see. Above all else, Jesus wanted them to know they could trust the Holy Spirit.

In the years to come, the disciples discovered that Jesus' words had been completely accurate. The Holy Spirit became their closest, most cherished Friend and personal Adviser.

The Holy Spirit is also our Comforter today. Everything He did for Jesus — and everything He did for the disciples and the Early Church — He still desires to do today. Two thousand years later, His name, His character, His behavior, His work, and His ministry have not changed.

As you go through the circumstances of life, the Holy Spirit is right alongside (*para*) to help you, assist you, defend you, teach you, advise you, and strengthen you with every step you take. (I highly recommend that you reread Chapter Six to make sure you understand the work of the Holy Spirit as our Comforter.)

2. The Holy Spirit Indwells Us

Even the Spirit of truth; whom the world cannot receive, because it seeth him not, neither knoweth him: but ye know him; for he dwelleth with you, and shall be in you.

— John 14:17

In John 20:22, Jesus breathed on the disciples and told them, "...Receive the Holy Spirit." The word "receive" comes from the Greek word *lambano*, which means *to receive something right now*. Because the word *lambano* is used here, it tells us something very important.

The word *lambano* means that Jesus was imparting the gift of the Holy Spirit to the disciples at that exact moment.

The Old Testament was coming to a grinding halt, and the New Testament was being initiated as the Spirit of God came to live inside the hearts of men for the first time in human history. Until this time, only Jesus had known the permanent indwelling of the Holy Spirit.

> As you go through the circumstances of life, the Holy Spirit is right alongside (*para*) to help you, assist you, defend you, teach you, advise you, and strengthen you with every step you take.

In the past, the Holy Spirit had temporarily come upon people to empower them for ministry and service, but He had never permanently lived inside a human being. Even the prophets, priests, and kings of the Old Testament never knew this glorious privilege. They knew the presence of the Holy Spirit only in a temporary way. On occasion, He came upon them to do something special, but then He lifted from them until the next time they needed to be specially empowered for service.

> When Jesus said the Holy Spirit would dwell within the disciples, He was making the most radical kind of statement any Jew could ever speak. He was declaring that for the first time in history, the Spirit of God was going to be present in the hearts of God's people on a permanent basis.

Therefore, when Jesus said the Holy Spirit would dwell within the disciples (*see* John 14:17), He was making the most radical kind of statement any Jew could ever speak. He was declaring that for the first time in history, the Spirit of God was going to be present in the hearts of God's people on a permanent basis.

In the Greek, the word "dwell" is the word *meno*. It means *to stay* or *to abide*. This is the picture of a person who has resolved that he is *never* going to move again. He has found the home of his dreams and is determined to stay there. He will not move, budge, flinch, or ever be forced to move out.

Jesus told us that the Holy Spirit's coming would mark a new time period for mankind when the Holy Spirit would come to permanently dwell in the hearts of all believers. Dwelling in men's hearts would not be temporary or fleeting in the way His presence had been in the Old Testament. This was to be a new covenant, based on better promises (*see* Hebrews 8:6). The Holy Spirit would never move, never waver, and never pack His bags to be transferred to another location.

Your heart was not meant to be a hotel! God never intended for the Holy Spirit to be just your guest. If the Holy Spirit were only a temporary guest, you couldn't develop a close partnership with Him — and a relationship of deep intimacy, knowledge, and trust.

But because the Holy Spirit has come to stay as a permanent Resident in your heart, this is a relationship well worth your time and energy. This Partner is with you for the rest of your life. That's another wonderful reason you should decide to get serious about cultivating your partnership with the Holy Spirit — starting today!

Think About It

Developing a partnership with the Spirit of God is no light matter, and it can't be done on an occasional basis according to our preferred schedule or what we deem is convenient. The Holy Spirit is the seal of our covenant relationship with Almighty God. It's an eternal transaction we willingly made with no escape clause. The Holy Spirit moved into our "temple," and He has no plans to move out. Yet it's possible to grieve Him and make Him uncomfortable with the choices we make at times.

As you look back at your past relationship with the Holy Spirit, what kind of "host" to His presence would you describe yourself to be? How comfortable have you made this divine Partner in His home called *you*? Have you often relegated Him to a "back sitting room," where He has waited for you to come enjoy times of intimacy and close fellowship together? Or has the Holy Spirit received the best of everything you could offer Him — including your pursuit to know His heart, to give him the firstfruits of your time, and to please Him in everything you do?

CHAPTER ELEVEN

THE HOLY SPIRIT TEACHES, REMINDS, AND TESTIFIES

*I*n the last chapter, we studied two works of the Holy Spirit in the lives of believers on the earth today:

1. The Holy Spirit comforts us.

2. The Holy Spirit indwells us.

The next three points we'll look at are things the Holy Spirit does *to help us mature spiritually* and *minister more effectively to others.* The Holy Spirit abides on the earth for the purposes I have already enumerated. But this inside-out work of the Spirit includes transforming our lives if we'll yield to Him as He *teaches* us, *reminds* us, and *testifies with* us.

3. The Holy Spirit Teaches Us

But the Comforter, which is the Holy Ghost, whom the Father will send in my name, he shall teach you all things.

— John 14:26

Jesus provides us with human teachers who are very helpful in equipping us with the truth we need to grow in the things of God. But first and foremost, He gives us the Teacher who will never fail us or lead us astray — the Holy Spirit.

Jesus said, "He shall not speak of himself; but whatsoever he shall hear, that shall he speak.... He shall take of mine, and shall show it unto you" (John 16:13,15). The Holy Spirit's role as a Teacher is to speak for Jesus Christ and not to speak on His own behalf. As Jesus did nothing unless He saw the Father doing it, likewise, the Holy Spirit does what He sees Jesus doing. He carries out the lordship of Jesus Christ in the Church.

Even the gifts of the Holy Spirit declare the testimony of Jesus Christ. That is why Paul told the Corinthians, "That in every thing ye are enriched by him, in all utterance, and in all knowledge; even as the testimony of Christ was confirmed in you" (1 Corinthians 1:5,6).

The Corinthian church was greatly endowed with spiritual gifts (*see* 1 Corinthians 1:7). Paul says they were "enriched" by them. The word "enriched" is the Greek word *ploutizo*, which means *to make extremely rich*. In today's vernacular, we might call this "filthy, stinking rich."

Paul said the Corinthian believers were particularly rich in "utterance and knowledge" — and, indeed, they came behind in no gift (*see* 1 Corinthians 1:5-7). Paul stated that the abundance of these gifts confirmed the testimony of Christ among them.

Before we go any further, let's look at the words "confirmed" and "testimony."

The word "confirmed" is the Greek word *bebaioo*, which means *to make firm, concrete, stable, or solid*. The word "testimony" is the Greek word *marturion*, which describes *a witness* or *a personal testimony so strong and valid that it could stand up to scrutiny in a court of law and pass the test with flying colors*.

The Corinthian church personally knew Jesus Christ as a Miracle-Worker and a Healer because they had seen the Holy

Spirit minister His miracle power in their midst. This firsthand witness confirmed and made that aspect of Jesus *concrete* in the Corinthian believers' hearts and minds. Jesus' testimony as a Prophet wasn't difficult for them to grasp, either, because they had experienced the gift of prophecy — words from Heaven spoken by the Spirit to encourage, exhort, and edify — so regularly in their midst.

The gifts of the Holy Spirit confirm the Person and work of Jesus Christ. Those gifts give testimony to the fact that He is still alive, still healing, and still working miracles today. By these marvelous gifts, the Holy Spirit teaches about and speaks on behalf of Jesus Christ.

The Holy Spirit also brings us the mind of Christ and the will of God. In regard to this divine responsibility, Paul wrote this: "Eye hath not seen, nor ear heard, neither have entered into the heart of man, the things which God hath prepared for them that love him. But God hath revealed them unto us by his Spirit: for the Spirit searches all things, yea, the deep things of God" (1 Corinthians 2:9,10,16).

> The gifts of the Holy Spirit confirm the Person and work of Jesus Christ. Those gifts give testimony to the fact that He is still alive, still healing, and still working miracles today.

Paul began this verse by talking about man's inability to understand the deep things of God by himself. It could have been translated, *"The heart of man could never dream, imagine, or conjure up the things that God has prepared for them who love Him."* The human heart couldn't dream up — even in its wildest imagination — the wonder of the blessings to be experienced along the path God has prepared for His children.

How then do we come to know and experience these blessings? Paul answered this question by saying, "But God hath revealed them unto us by his Spirit…" (v. 10). The word "revealed" is the word *apokalupto*, which means *to unveil, to reveal,* or *to uncover.* It is actually a picture of something that is veiled or hidden, and then *suddenly* its veil or covering is removed. As a result, what was hidden for so long now comes into plain view. And God does all of this *by His Spirit.*

The Holy Spirit lifts the cover and removes the veil that blocks our view of God's promises to us. As He opens the eyes of our spirits to previously veiled truths, He continues to teach us the Word of God, which ultimately testifies to the lordship of Jesus Christ in our lives.

Furthermore, the Holy Spirit is the One who inspired the Bible. Second Timothy 3:16 says, "All scripture is given by inspiration of God…." The Greek word for "inspiration" is *theopneustos,* which literally means *God-breathed, God-inspired,* or *breathed into by God.* The Holy Spirit was the divine Agent who provided the inspired utterance from the heart of the Father to the hearts of those called to write down the words.

The work of the Holy Spirit to inspire and direct the writing of Scripture doesn't pertain only to the New Testament. Second Peter 1:21 reveals that the Holy Spirit anointed and inspired the Old Testament writers as well: "For the prophecy came not in old time by the will of man: but holy men of God spake as they were moved by the Holy Ghost."

As the Inspirer and Author of Old and New Testament Scripture, the Holy Spirit also becomes the ultimate Teacher. No one knows the Bible better. No one can teach it better than the One who inspired it and imparted it to the hearts and minds of men so that it could be recorded, or written down. And He's still imparting it to the hearts and minds of men today. That's the Holy Spirit — our great Teacher!

4. The Holy Spirit Reminds Us

He shall teach you all things, and bring all things to your remembrance, whatsoever I have said unto you.

— John 14:26

Have you ever wondered, *How did the disciples remember everything Jesus taught them?*

Think about it! With all the thousands, even millions of words the disciples heard Jesus speak, how did they ever remember them all correctly? This would require great intellect and a remarkable memory — or someone who recorded everything Jesus said, *as He said it*, when He was on this earth.

This leads us to the fourth responsibility God gave to the Holy Spirit — *to bring to our remembrance all the things Jesus did, said, and taught.*

The Bible gives an example of the reminding work of the Holy Spirit at Jesus' triumphal entry into Jerusalem when the people were joyfully proclaiming, "...Hosanna: Blessed is the King of Israel that cometh in the name of the Lord" (John 12:13).

At the time this was happening, the disciples didn't realize Old Testament Scripture was being fulfilled before their eyes. John 12:16 goes on to say, "These things understood not his disciples at the first: but when Jesus was glorified, then remembered they that things were written of him, and that they had done these things unto him."

So when John later sat down to write this gospel, he had the inspiration and insight to quote Zechariah 9:9, saying, "And Jesus, when he had found a young ass, sat thereon; as it is written,

Fear not, daughter of Sion: behold, thy King cometh, sitting on an ass's colt" (John 12:14,15).

After the Holy Spirit was poured out upon the apostles and the others at Pentecost, one of the ways He taught them about Jesus was by tying Old Testament Scripture into events they had experienced with Jesus. Many things that had not been clear or had not made sense to them while Jesus was on earth were being explained and defined as the Holy Spirit led them to Old Testament verses. And as He inspired the apostles to write the New Testament, He clarified and revealed to them the significance of the Old Testament in connection with what was happening before their eyes.

Today all Scripture is written and, according to Revelation 22:18 and 19, there is nothing we can add to it. There will be no new revelations about the life of Christ. Everything the Holy Spirit wants us to know about it, He has already told us. That doesn't mean we've exhausted and understood everything from Scripture that there is to glean. It simply means that the Holy Scripture has been presented to us in its entirety. There will be no "new" revelations of the life of Christ outside the bounds of what has been written.

One of the most remarkable things about the Early Church was the four gospel writers' fantastic ability to remember what Jesus said and did. Yet some modern scholars try to discredit the gospels by declaring that they are merely a product of the imperfect memories of the disciples. They argue that the gospels don't contain the actual words of Jesus. But those scholars have forgotten that one aspect of the work of the Holy Spirit was and still is to remind Jesus' followers of everything Jesus said and did.

What we have in the gospels is exactly what Jesus said and did. They were written as the Holy Spirit put the gospel writers in remembrance. How marvelous and fantastic it truly is to see how the Holy Spirit illuminated their minds to recall vivid details from Jesus' life and ministry! It is due to this wonderful work of the Holy Spirit that we have the books of Matthew, Mark, Luke, and John in our Bibles today.

We can never claim ignorance as our excuse for doing wrong, for forgetting what we should do, or for not knowing Scripture. The Holy Spirit dwells within us, and His purpose is to give us exactly what we need when we need it. He is ever ready to help us think and do what is right at all times. When our partnership with the Holy Spirit is strong, we can lean upon Him the moment our memory fails us because it is His responsibility to remind us of the Word of God.

We might be in the midst of a situation in which we don't know what to do. But the Holy Spirit is always alongside us to reach into the Word of God, illuminate the exact verse or truth we need, and put us in remembrance of it at just the right moment.

Perhaps this responsibility of the Holy Spirit is best illustrated in parts of the world where the Bible is illegal. Communist governments have strictly forbidden the printing and distribution of the Word of God for years, yet underground believers in those nations know the Scripture well. In many nations of the world, the Bible is still illegal, but you can also be sure that the believers in those nations know the Word of God.

> The Holy Spirit dwells within us, and His purpose is to give us exactly what we need when we need it. He is ever ready to help us think and do what is right at all times.

For more than a quarter of a century, my family and I have lived in the former Soviet Union. Up until the fall of the Iron Curtain, the Bible had been forbidden there for more than 70 years. When I first came to live in this region of the world, I was in awe of the leaders and entire church congregations I met who had lived through the Soviet years and had owned only one Bible through the years. Sometimes it was a hand-copied version with torn and tattered pages from decades of use. Those yellowed, ragged pages of the Word of God meant everything to them.

What respect those believers had for the Word of God! Not having the Bible made them cherish it even more. Those who actually owned Bibles held them close to their hearts. They would never lay one on the ground, place something on top of it, such as a coffee cup — or even leave it sitting on a chair unguarded.

It is the most amazing thing to see people who have had limited access to the Bible and yet know it so well. They can quote it and remember it better than people in free countries who have several Bibles in their houses and the opportunity to read them every morning and every night! (In light of this, I think those who have been blessed with multiple Bibles in their homes and yet don't know the Word of God need to give some serious thought to their lives.)

There is only one explanation for this amazing retention of Scripture in believers' hearts in closed countries: *The Holy Spirit.* He is doing exactly what Jesus said He would do — putting those believers in remembrance of the Word of God. That is one of the Holy Spirit's responsibilities as our Partner in this world.

5. The Holy Spirit Testifies With Us

But when the Comforter is come, whom I will send to you from the Father, even the Spirit of truth, which proceedeth from the Father, he shall testify of me.

— John 15:26

As I mentioned earlier, when I was young, I used to despise witnessing. I loved Jesus with all my heart. But getting in the car to go knock on doors and talk to people I'd never met before in my life — and then to read a ten-page tract to them that they weren't interested in hearing — was *not* my idea of having a good time! Other church members must have had the same problem, because our pastor constantly had to beg and coax our congregation to participate in Sunday school visitation and evangelism.

Nevertheless, I knew I was supposed to witness for Christ. The trouble was that being a witness wasn't what I *was* — it was a job I *did*. I can remember piling into my Sunday school teacher's car and looking at the list of names we were to visit. I distinctly recall the sinking feeling I had on the inside as I thought about knocking on all those doors. I felt so powerless, defeated, and joyless as we went to fulfill our witnessing duty.

Although many believers would never want to admit it, they have felt the same way about witnessing too. The truth is, there is no witness and no testimony without the work of the Holy Spirit. Believers must have the Holy Spirit's help as they testify. That is why Jesus gave the fifth point about the Holy Spirit's responsibility to us: "...He shall testify of me...."

The Holy Spirit's testimony may take the form of giving you a new revelation regarding Jesus Christ for your own spiritual growth and to minister to someone else's specific need as He leads you. Or He may direct you to people who are lost and then provide the words you need to share with them about Jesus' redemptive work. Either way, the Holy Spirit loves to testify of Jesus because of His deep love, adoration, and affection for Him.

When Jesus told the disciples to stay in Jerusalem, He was giving them divine strategy to follow that would equip them in their service to Him. He said, "But ye shall receive power, *after* that the Holy Ghost is come upon you: and ye shall be witnesses unto me both in Jerusalem, and in all of Judea, and in Samaria, and unto the uttermost part of the earth" (Acts 1:8).

Notice Jesus said the disciples would be witnesses "after" the Holy Spirit came upon them. To witness and testify powerfully about the resurrected Christ, supernatural power is required. Hence, without the Holy Spirit's assistance, it is almost impossible to testify with this supernatural confidence about Jesus Christ.

Before the Day of Pentecost, the disciples were similar to many Christians today. Rather than forcefully advancing upon the world, they were hiding behind closed doors. Unlike the great spiritual army they were supposed to be, they were simply maintaining and "holing up" in the Upper Room.

Jesus said the Holy Spirit came to testify, but not until Acts 2 did the disciples comprehend the greatness of the Spirit's ability to do that. The witness of Jesus Christ literally *blasted* out of their mouths as they hit the streets of Jerusalem, fully yielded to the Person of the Holy Spirit. In addition to supernaturally declaring "the wonderful works of God" in other languages (Acts 2:11), the 120 proclaimed the Word of God intelligently in their own language to a people they had been afraid of the day before!

After Peter received the infilling of the Holy Spirit, he boldly proclaimed, "Ye men of Israel, hear these words; Jesus of Nazareth, a man approved by God among you by miracles and wonders and signs, which God did by him in the midst of you.... Ye have taken, and by wicked hands have crucified whom God hath raised up, having loosed the pains of death.... Therefore being by the right hand of God exalted..." (Acts 2:22,23,33).

This was a supernatural proclamation! This was supernatural evangelism!

Now, there is nothing wrong with preplanned evangelism, door-to-door visitation, or evangelism programs that teach us the basics of witnessing. But when those programs replace the presence and power of the Holy Spirit, they negate what God intended witnessing to be.

True, biblical witnessing involves yielding to the leading and power of the Holy Spirit to eternally impact a life with the truth of Jesus Christ. Therefore, witnessing that occurs separate from this power becomes a dry, dead, non-gratifying religious work.

True witnessing or testifying of Jesus Christ can only be done in relation to the power of the resurrection. This is what Acts 4:33 refers to when it says, "And with great power gave the apostles witness of the resurrection of the Lord Jesus: and great grace was upon them all." Even under the Old Covenant, God's people understood that they could not fulfill spiritual tasks by natural means. For example, Zechariah 4:6 says, "…Not by might, nor by power, but *by my spirit*, saith the Lord of hosts."

> **Biblical witnessing involves yielding to the leading and power of the Holy Spirit to eternally impact a life with the truth of Jesus Christ.**

So why lean on your own understanding when it comes to witnessing? Why reduce the power of the resurrection to a mere program? The Holy Spirit was sent to testify of Jesus. No one knows how to testify better than He does!

If you are afraid to witness as I was, open your heart to the partnership of the Holy Spirit and let Him take responsibility for testifying about Jesus through you. As you surrender your heart and mind to the Spirit's control, witnessing will change from stressful drudgery to a joyful, rewarding, and exciting adventure!

THINK ABOUT IT

When Jesus gave the disciples their mandate, He gave them a divine sequence to follow (*see* Acts 1:4,8): They were to prayerfully wait in Jerusalem; the Holy Spirit would come upon them; they would receive power; and *then* they would be His witnesses. God's higher ways often don't make sense to man's natural mind. He is a strategic God who sees the end from the beginning and orders our steps accordingly to fit the larger picture of His great plan for mankind. Then He tasks the Holy Spirit to *reveal* His higher ways to us.

That means you will receive guidance from the Spirit of God at times that seems illogical or at least "out-of-sequence" according to your way of thinking. Those are often the key moments you need to heed the prompting of the Holy Spirit and simply obey. Think of an example of one of these key moments in your own life and consider your response to the Holy Spirit's "illogical prompting." How did your response impact the ultimate outcome of that situation?

CHAPTER TWELVE

THE HOLY SPIRIT CONVICTS AND CONVINCES

The Holy Spirit has a complementary ministry to our own consciences, both *convicting* us of sin and *convincing* us of righteousness (*see* John 16:8-10). In this chapter, we'll look at these two crucial aspects of the Holy Spirit's work and responsibility to us.

6. The Holy Spirit Convicts Us

> **And when he is come, he will reprove the world...of sin, because they believe not on me.**
>
> **— John 16:8,9**

Do you remember when you were a child and you did something wrong, but you thought no one was watching what you were doing? Then you got caught. Do you remember how it felt, realizing someone had been watching you all along? What a feeling of horror and dread — to be caught in the middle of the act!

You couldn't lie your way out of such a situation, because someone had been watching you the whole time. You were unmistakably guilty and couldn't escape facing your sin. Can you remember what it was like to feel so exposed?

This is what sinners feel the first time the Holy Spirit convicts them of sin. It is amazing how long sinners can live without conviction or sorrow for their behavior — nearly numb to the wrongness of their actions. The Bible says sin has made them to be hardhearted, spiritually blind, and past feeling (*see* Ephesians 4:18,19). Compound this with the fact that they are spiritually dead and therefore insensitive and non-responsive to God, and you find out why lost people can do some of the terrible things they do over and over again.

But that numb, hardhearted spiritual state can change instantaneously when the Holy Spirit touches the human soul and exposes its sinful condition. Awakened by the Spirit to see his true spiritual condition, a sinner feels exposed, naked, embarrassed, and *confronted*.

Jesus said the Holy Spirit would reprove people in the world of sin in this way in order to bring them to the saving knowledge of Jesus Christ. The word "reprove" is the Greek word *elegcho*. It means *to expose, to convict, or to cross-examine for the purpose of conviction*, as in convicting a lawbreaker in a court of law.

As the Holy Spirit enables the sinner to truly hear the Word of God for the first time, that Word is so razor sharp that it penetrates his soul until he feels as if he has been cross-examined on a witness stand. Finally, the court is adjourned, the verdict is announced, and he is declared guilty. That is a manifestation of the work of the Holy Spirit to convict sinners of their lost condition.

The whole world stands guilty before God (*see* Romans 3:19), but the whole world doesn't realize it is guilty. Jesus taught that "no man can come unto me, except the Father draw him" (*see* John 6:44). This drawing unto the Father is done through the work of the Holy Spirit. Jesus reminded us of this truth when He said, "And when he is come, he will reprove the world of sin..."

(John 16:8). Without the work of the Holy Spirit to expose our sinful condition, we would still be in darkness today, eternally lost and without God.

It is frustrating to share Christ with family and friends and to feel as if you are "hitting a brick wall." You share, talk, and plead with them to receive Christ, yet it seems they just can't hear what you are saying. Even though they know they are sinners, they don't seem to be convicted by this knowledge. Ignoring the ultimate outcome of their dangerous spiritual condition, they press on — either numb or ignorant of the degree of spiritual decay in their lives.

The Bible says the lost person is "...dead in trespasses and sins" (Ephesians 2:1). Dead people don't feel anything! They especially don't feel the conviction of sin. It requires a special, supernatural work of the Holy Spirit to rouse the human consciousness to the reality of its sinful condition.

How can you make a dead man see? You can't, for he is dead. How can you cause a dead man to feel? How can you convince a spiritually dead man that he needs to change?

It is impossible for a dead man to respond. But what is impossible with man is possible with God (*see* Luke 18:27)! Thanks to the Holy Spirit's call that touched our souls, we were awakened to our sinfulness, and the Spirit beckoned us to Christ. Once we were brought to this excruciating place of undeniable conviction and recognized that we were sinners, the Holy Spirit then invited us to come to God. At that divine moment, our souls heard Him say, in effect, "Awake thou that sleepest, and arise from the dead, and Christ shall give thee light" (Ephesians 5:14).

What a miracle that God raised our spirits from spiritual death to spiritual life! There is no greater miracle! This convicting work of the Holy Spirit is the first thing the Holy Spirit ever does in our lives — but it is certainly not the last.

The Holy Spirit continues His convicting work in our lives as believers, letting us know when we have missed the mark. Then it's up to us how we respond to Him.

> **What a miracle that God raised our spirits from spiritual death to spiritual life! There is no greater miracle!**

And we need to know how important it is that we *do* respond to the Holy Spirit when He convicts us. It's possible for us to violate our "built-in" inner voice of conscience in certain areas and to override the Holy Spirit's voice in our hearts to the point that we're no longer sensitive to His convicting work in our lives in those areas.

But it never has to be that way in our lives as believers. It's always a matter of choice.

7. The Holy Spirit Convinces Us

And when he is come, he will reprove...of righteousness, because I go to my Father, and ye see me no more.

John 16:8,10

Before we proceed with the *convincing* ministry of the Holy Spirit, let's review the previous six aspects of the Holy Spirit's work in our lives that we already covered:

1. The Holy Spirit comforts us.

2. The Holy Spirit indwells us.

3. The Holy Spirit teaches us.

4. The Holy Spirit reminds us.

5. The Holy Spirit testifies with us.

6. The Holy Spirit convicts us.

In verses 8 and 10, Jesus said about the Holy Spirit, "And when he is come, he will reprove...of righteousness, because I go to my Father, and ye see me no more." In this section, we're going to talk about the convincing power and ministry of the Holy Spirit.

Have you ever complimented someone who then argued with you, rejecting your compliment and essentially questioning your judgment in the matter? For example, rather than thanking you after you said the person looked as if he had lost weight, he responded by telling you how fat he is.

"Well, I've gained a lot of weight, and I look so fat now. I wish you could have seen me three months ago when I really looked good! I don't look as good now." This is the equivalent of throwing the compliment back in your face. It would be far more polite to be gracious and say, "Thank you. I'm so glad you noticed. I appreciate your telling me I look better."

Here is another example. Someone sings a solo during a church service that deeply stirs your heart. At the end of the service, you make your way through the congregation to find the soloist to tell that person how much his song ministered to you. He responds, "Thanks for the compliment, but I thought I did a horrible job tonight. I can't believe I sang so badly. I don't know how you got anything out of it."

It's rude to respond that way to a compliment. It is rejecting the love, admiration, and appreciation God is expressing through someone else to encourage you. It's the same as saying, "I appreciate your giving me this compliment, but we both know it isn't true, so you don't have to say it." In effect, you're telling the person who is complimenting you that he is a liar!

Of course, if you've ever done this, you probably didn't intend to be ill-mannered. Nevertheless, you must learn to accept a compliment. When someone compliments you, don't try to convince the person of how bad you look, how terribly you performed, and so on.

But here's the ironic part: We do this to God every day! This is why Jesus told us about a very special responsibility the Holy Spirit has concerning our lives: *The Holy Spirit comes to convince us of righteousness.*

Second Corinthians 5:21 declares, "For he hath made him to be sin for us, who knew no sin; that we might be made the righteousness of God in him." What a wonderful work God did for us! He sent Jesus to die in our place and to take our sin upon Himself. He exerted all of His mighty power to raise Jesus from the dead and then seated Him at His own right hand. Then He sent the Holy Spirit to live in us so we could become "the righteousness of God in him" (2 Corinthians 5:21)!

Yet if there is any subject in Scripture that Christians will argue about, it is this question of righteousness. Most Christians are so conscious of their old sinful nature (which still abides in their flesh, but not in their brand-new, recreated spirit) that they can't embrace the truth that they have been declared righteous. Tell them they are good, and they respond by telling you how bad they are.

Sinful nature always clings to what is the worst and most negative. It will always gravitate *downward*, never *upward*. That is the nature of the mind that is not under the control of the Holy Spirit.

This is why lost people can do such inhumane things. Even for the believer, the sinful flesh — if not mortified by the sanctifying power of the Holy Spirit — will ultimately follow its negative leanings all the way to the grave.

If you become abandoned to your flesh, you'll never believe a good report, you'll never believe that God is doing a good work in you, and you'll certainly never believe that you have been made "the righteousness of God in Christ."

Negative, base, sinful thinking has been a part of our humanity for so long that it requires a special convincing work of the Holy Spirit to make us realize the miraculous work God has wrought in us. This special work of the Holy Spirit to convince us of our rightstanding with God is crucial. Otherwise, when God says, "You're My child. I have made you righteous. You are beautiful to Me," our negatively charged mind and emotions will retort, "It's not so! I'm unworthy. I'm unholy. I'm so pitiful!"

Again, this is like throwing the "compliment" back in God's face! Imagine it: He put forth His best work to redeem us and make us "new creations," yet too often we have nothing good to say about ourselves in honor of that work (*see* 2 Corinthians 5:17).

The Bible tells us that we are "his workmanship, created in Christ Jesus" (Ephesians 2:10). Another translation of that verse could be, *"We are a product of His very own, marvelously created in Christ Jesus — that is, created under the influence and control of His divine power."*

> **Negative, base, sinful thinking has been a part of our humanity for so long that it requires a special convincing work of the Holy Spirit to make us realize the miraculous work God has wrought in us.**

This is powerful, life-changing truth, but it takes the Holy Spirit to move this truth from a believer's head to his heart. Just as the Holy Spirit must *convict* the sinner of his lost condition, He also must *convince* the believer of his new rightstanding with God.

We are so negative in our old, fleshly nature that it takes a supernatural work of God to cause us to truly comprehend our new condition in Christ Jesus. This realization is just as supernatural as the moment our unregenerate spirit man recognized he was lost. Only this time, we are being awakened to the fact that we are righteous!

I can remember when the Holy Spirit woke me up to this truth many years ago. Driving down the street, feeling totally unrighteous, I was listening to an audio teaching on righteousness. Suddenly my mind began to grasp what I was hearing. It was as if someone took blinders off my eyes and earplugs out of my ears.

For the first time, I was seeing and hearing the truth about my new righteousness in Christ Jesus. This truth was going straight to my heart by the power of the Holy Spirit! I heard it. I understood it. My inward man leaped for joy when the Spirit of God illumined my understanding about righteousness. He convinced me of the truth, and I was set free!

If you struggle with your self-image and feelings of condemnation, you need the Holy Spirit to do His convincing work in your life. Only He can open your eyes to see who you have become eternally in Christ Jesus.

Once your eyes have been opened and you truly grasp that God sees you as righteous, you will never again throw the truth back in His face and argue with Him. From that point on when the Holy Spirit reminds you that you have been declared righteous, you will cry out with joy, "Thank You! That's exactly what I am!"

You don't have to keep being negative about yourself all the time. You don't have to beat yourself over the head, constantly telling yourself how unworthy you are. In fact, you actually insult the power in the redemptive work of Jesus when you do that! Jesus Christ *made* you worthy when He went to the Cross on your behalf and shed His own precious blood. He *made* you righteous! He *made* you a new creation in Him.

> My inward man leaped for joy when the Spirit of God illumined my understanding about righteousness. He convinced me of the truth, and I was set free!

Why is this so important? Because if you don't have a grasp of this God-given righteousness, which is the only basis for a good self-image, you will never know who you really are in Him and what your true purpose in life is.

Furthermore, a negative self-image will inhibit your ability to pray with confidence and trust God to answer you. It will keep you from living a life free of guilt and condemnation.

A false understanding of righteousness is that it is bestowed only after you go to Heaven but has no part of your life on earth. This misunderstanding causes a cloud of guilt and condemnation to hang over you for the rest of your life, hindering your ability to walk in the joy and victory of the Lord.

Perhaps you can better see now why the convincing work of the Holy Spirit is not an option for those who want to progress as mature Christians. The Holy Spirit takes this responsibility seriously for good reason. It is an absolute necessity.

THINK ABOUT IT

Too often we let ourselves get caught up in a familiar pattern of insecure, self-condemning thoughts without considering how that affects the Holy Spirit who dwells within us. The very Savior He was sent to magnify in our lives is the One whose redemptive work we're insulting when we allow the enemy to torment us with that destructive thought pattern.

Can you think of times in your life when these types of thoughts have bombarded your own mind? Did you make the conscious decision to set aside time to commune with the Holy Spirit and the Word of God? Every time you choose to make *that* your response to the enemy's attack on your mind, the Holy Spirit will help you replace those fear-based thoughts with *the Father's* thoughts about you. And as you determine to make this your lifelong response every time thoughts of insecurity and self-condemnation try to resurface, you open the way for the Holy Spirit to fully *convince* you of who you are in Christ so you can walk in the fullness of all He has created you to be.

CHAPTER THIRTEEN

THE HOLY SPIRIT GUIDES, REVEALS, AND HELPS US WORSHIP

*I*n Chapter Ten, I introduced ten aspects of the Holy Spirit's ministry that is available to us as believers. The last three we'll cover from John 14-16 concern *the Holy Spirit's work through our actions.*

Let's study these carefully, for these particular aspects of the Holy Spirit's work in our lives are key to cultivating intimacy with Him as He works in us to help us fulfill our God-ordained destiny.

8. The Holy Spirit Guides Us

Have you ever asked, *What am I supposed to do with my life? What direction am I supposed to take? How can I know for certain that I am doing what God wants me to do?*

These are difficult questions to answer at times, and we have all asked them over and over again. Although the Bible contains God's revelation of Himself to man, it doesn't always answer our specific questions about the details of daily life — for example, what job we should take or what person we should marry.

The Bible gives us guiding principles for our choices in life, such as to abstain from the appearance of evil (*see* 1 Thessalonians 5:22) or not to be yoked with unbelievers (*see* 2 Corinthians 6:14). From these principles, we can make the decisions not to take a job as a bartender, for example, nor marry a person who hasn't committed his or her life to Jesus Christ.

We must commit ourselves to study and memorize the Word of God, hiding it in our hearts so we will not sin against God (*see* Psalm 119:11). Then because we are guided by God's Word, we will make fewer mistakes in our choices as we move along in life.

Nevertheless, as wonderful and holy as these guiding principles are, they don't tell us specifically which job to take or what person to marry! They don't tell us which city to live in — or even which *country* — and they don't tell us what church to get involved in and what ministries to get behind and support. Sometimes we need guidance, direction, and answers that are not written in the Scriptures, and Jesus said the Holy Spirit would give us this kind of guidance: "...He will guide you into all the truth..." (John 16:13).

Divine guidance in our daily lives is one of the biggest challenges we face in the Christian life. Thus, we have been provided with another tremendous responsibility of the Holy Spirit — *telling us what to do and when to do it every step of the way.*

This guiding work of the Holy Spirit was crucial to the Early Church. Early believers trusted the leadership of the Holy Spirit to guide them in the formation of doctrine, the selection of leaders, where to minister, whom to send on certain missionary journeys, etc.

It's interesting to note that before the Holy Spirit was poured out upon the disciples in Acts 2, they tried to make a big decision without His help. They decided to choose a replacement for

Judas, who had killed himself after he betrayed Jesus. They had narrowed it down to two men, "...Joseph called Barsabas, who was surnamed Justus, and Matthias" (Acts 1:23).

Remember that Jesus, just before He ascended, had instructed them to go directly to Jerusalem and tarry until the Holy Ghost came upon them (*see* Luke 24:49). In essence, He was saying, "Go to Jerusalem, and don't do one single, solitary thing or make any decisions whatsoever until you are endowed with power from the Holy Spirit!"

The disciples went to Jerusalem and waited, but then they seemed to get a little impatient and started to look for something to do. Peter had the notion that someone should replace Judas. After they came up with two candidates, this was what happened:

> **And they prayed, and said, Thou, Lord, which knowest the hearts of all men, shew whether of these two thou hast chosen, That he may take part of this ministry and apostleship, from which Judas by transgression fell, that he might go to his own place. And they gave forth their lots; and the lot fell upon Matthias; And they prayed, and said, Thou, Lord, which knowest the hearts of all men, show whether of these two thou hast chosen, that he may take part of this ministry and apostleship, and he was numbered with the eleven apostles.**
>
> **— Acts 1:24-26**

The Bible says they "cast lots" to decide between the two men. In other words, they made the decision by a roll of the dice!

Contrast this instance of Jesus' disciples seeking guidance with those that occurred after the Holy Spirit was given on the Day of Pentecost, and you will find an incredibly significant difference. For one thing, never again did the apostles use a "roll of the dice" to make a decision.

Let's look at a few of these examples from the book of Acts. You will see that in addition to guiding us into the truth of the Bible, the Holy Spirit also has a guiding hand in the daily affairs of our lives if we will allow Him that place in our lives.

In Acts 13:2, we read, "As they ministered to the Lord, and fasted, the Holy Ghost said, Separate me Barnabas and Saul for the work whereunto I have called them." This marked the point where the apostle Paul was sent out on his first missionary journey. He was to accompany Barnabas, who had been spending the last few years discipling him.

In Acts 15, the apostles and elders in Jerusalem sent Paul and Barnabas to Antioch with a letter containing the following message: "For it seemed good to the Holy Ghost, and to us, to lay upon you no greater burden than these necessary things" (v. 28).

At that time, there was a great doctrinal dispute going on in the Church regarding how much of the Old Testament Law should be adhered to by Gentile believers — such as circumcision, keeping the Sabbath, and so forth. In this letter, the elders gave the saints at Antioch the conclusions they had reached in agreement with the Holy Spirit.

Just a short time later, Paul was planning to travel to several different places to preach the Gospel, but the Holy Spirit told him not to go. "Now when they had gone throughout Phrygia and the region of Galatia, and were forbidden of the Holy Ghost to preach the word in Asia, after they were come to Mysia, they assayed to go into Bithynia: but the Spirit suffered them not" (Acts 16:6,7).

All of these accounts in the book of Acts say one very important thing to us: *We cannot know what to do, where to go, with whom to go, and when to go without the guidance and direction of the Holy Spirit.*

We also see that the Holy Spirit can lead us in two ways — by saying *yes* or by saying *no*! He will try to stop us from doing something that looks good to us but is either a trap of the enemy or not God's will. Conversely, He will open a door of opportunity and give us total peace to walk through it, even in the midst of adversity.

What a relief and security it gives us to know that God the Father has given the Holy Spirit the responsibility of leading us, guiding us, and even warning us away from certain people, places, and situations. This is His job. And if we will listen to Him and obey what He tells us to do, we will ultimately fulfill our divine calling and walk out our part in the plans and purposes of God.

9. The Holy Spirit Reveals to Us

> **For he shall not speak of himself; but whatsoever he shall hear, that shall he speak: and he will shew you things to come.**
>
> **— John 16:13**

We have already discussed how one of the Holy Spirit's responsibilities is to represent Jesus to us and to be our communication link with Him. Jesus said that the Holy Spirit would not say or do anything He didn't hear or see from Jesus, just as Jesus didn't say or do anything He didn't hear or see from the Father.

The Holy Spirit will most often reveal things to us during times of prayer. And whatever the Holy Spirit reveals to us, we can be sure that it is coming straight from the throne room of God. We can trust what He is saying to us, whether it

> What a relief and security it gives us to know that God the Father has given the Holy Spirit the responsibility of leading us, guiding us, and even warning us away from certain people, places, and situations.

has to do with how we are ordering our lives, which job to take, whom to marry, how to deal with our children, or the nature of our divine calling and purpose.

One of the most widely quoted scriptures for the Holy Spirit's involvement in prayer, and one of my personal favorites, is Romans 8:26: "Likewise the Spirit also helpeth our infirmities: for we know not what we should pray for as we ought." This verse is packed with nuggets from the Greek that will sharpen our understanding about the Holy Spirit's active role in revealing what we need to know in our daily lives.

Have you ever experienced a time when you didn't know what to pray for yourself or someone else? Or have you ever been in a terrible dilemma, and you didn't know how to get out of it? Maybe you've said, "Lord, the desire of my heart is so deep, but my mind is so confused. I'm not even sure if I know what the desire of my heart really *is*! Lord, please help me pray."

Those are times when we especially thank God for Romans 8:26. This verse shows the Holy Spirit's responsibility to reveal to us the will or wisdom of God for our lives through prayer.

The most important thing to realize is that prayer is not something we do by ourselves. Prayer is a two-way conversation between us and the Lord, an outgrowth and manifestation of the intimacy and partnership we share with Him. During this intimate time of communication, the Holy Spirit reveals Jesus' perspective on certain situations and what He wants us to do or not do.

The very first part of Romans 8:26 says, "Likewise the Spirit also helpeth...." What does that mean? The Greek word for "helpeth" is a compound word. The first part of the word means *to do something in conjunction with somebody else*. The second part means *to receive.* Together they convey the meaning *to take hold of something with somebody else.*

The word "helpeth" conveys the idea of real partnership and cooperation between two individuals who are working together toward the same end. It is not the idea of one person doing one part of the job and another person doing another part. Rather, it carries the idea of *two intimate friends or partners together giving all of their joint resources to solve a problem, overcome an obstacle, defeat an enemy, handle a difficult situation, or understand a dilemma.*

> **Prayer is a two-way conversation between us and the Lord, an outgrowth and manifestation of the intimacy and partnership we share with Him.**

In this kind of partnership in prayer, you and the Holy Spirit together will reach that supernatural peace that passes all understanding. He will reveal to you how to think, what to say, and what to do about a matter.

Let's continue with Romans 8:26: "Likewise the Spirit also helpeth our *infirmities*...." The word "infirmities" is a Greek word that really should be translated *weaknesses.* This word describes people who are *weak, sick,* or *broken down in their bodies, minds, or emotions.* Frequently, it is used to describe those who have lost their sense of spiritual well-being and strength, often without even knowing why.

The Holy Spirit will reveal your infirmities and help you with them. Some things are obvious, but even obvious problems may contain something hidden that only the Holy Spirit knows. That's why you have to depend on the Holy Spirit's leading and direction in all things, just as Jesus did during His ministry on earth.

For example, the Holy Spirit may be warning you of an upcoming financial attack of the enemy. He may be trying to tell you the reason you haven't been healed of an illness so you can make adjustments and be healed. He may want to show you that you've been overtaken by a fault, such as an addiction or an obsession, and that you need to be set free. He may be urging you to set aside some things that are weights in your life and are holding you back from fulfilling your destiny.

Whatever the Holy Spirit is revealing to you, you can be sure He will live up to *His* responsibility. He will come right alongside you and tell you everything you need to know to turn your problem into a victory!

"Likewise the Spirit also helpeth our infirmities: for we know not what we should pray for as we ought." In the literal Greek, that last part simply means, *"...We do not have the know-how when it comes to prayer."* The most skilled and experienced intercessors are the ones who, no matter what the situation, will turn immediately to their most intimate Partner and Friend, the Holy Spirit, and make certain they are on the right track in prayer.

> **Whatever the Holy Spirit is revealing to you, you can be sure He will live up to His responsibility. He will come right alongside you and tell you everything you need to know to turn your problem into a victory!**

All of us are occasionally confronted with a crisis or a decision about which we don't know how to pray. This is part of our human, limited condition, and it is this "infirmity" that the Holy Spirit comes to remove. He comes to give us the know-how. He makes up for whatever we lack.

"...For we know not what we should pray for as we ought." The word "what" is an interesting word in the Greek. It means *the very exact little thing*. We don't know the fine points, the details, or the real root of the problem with which we are dealing. We're simply not able to see all the facts or have a comprehensive view. But the Holy Spirit *does* have a very precise, accurate view.

For example, we need divine guidance and help to locate and handle all the fine little details of the fiery darts the enemy is bombarding us with. We need the mind of Christ to deal with them — and the mind of Christ is what we receive as we trust our Partner in prayer, obeying His instructions, saying what He says, and doing what He does.

I'm so grateful that God has given the Holy Spirit this responsibility of helping us pray, since every one of us is a flawed human being with quirks and blind spots. Whenever we're in the dark about anything, our first and foremost Prayer Partner will reveal to us whatever we need to know for whatever we're going through.

10. The Holy Spirit Helps Us Worship

He shall glorify me: for he shall receive of mine, and shall shew it unto you.

— John 16:14

In this verse of Scripture, Jesus is telling us that one of the responsibilities of the Holy Spirit is *to glorify Him*. The Holy Spirit is an invisible Spirit, and the vessel He chooses to glorify Jesus through is the one in which He lives — *you!*

Just how does the Holy Spirit fulfill His responsibility to glorify Jesus Christ through you? First, He can heal the sick, cast out demons, and lead lost people to the saving knowledge of Jesus Christ through you. These acts certainly glorify Jesus in a magnificent way.

But when we're talking about enjoying communion with the Holy Spirit, we come to another more intimate and equally important way in which the Holy Spirit glorifies Jesus through you — *in acts of praise and worship.*

I remember the first Charismatic prayer meeting I attended as a young teenager, which was held in a Charismatic believer's home. I didn't understand everything that happened that evening, but the one thing that captivated me and ultimately attracted me to continue with the Charismatic movement was the praise and worship.

> **Whenever we're in the dark about anything, our first and foremost Prayer Partner will reveal to us whatever we need to know for whatever we're going through.**

During that time of praise and worship among those who were filled with the Holy Spirit, I experienced the presence of the Lord more than I ever had before. It was as though He were standing so close that I could feel His breath on my face and sense the warmth of His body.

In this intimate, personal time of lifting our hands and hearts to God, I became "drunk" with the presence of Jesus. As I left that meeting, I found myself thinking about praising and worshiping the Lord and making melody in my heart to Him. I was like a child who had just tasted ice cream for the first time — I wanted more and more and more. I wanted every aspect of Jesus to come pouring through me in a brand-new, powerful, and personal way.

As I look back on that experience now, I can see why all I could think about and long for was more of Jesus. I had been filled with the Holy Spirit, and that's all *He* thinks about and longs for! All the Holy Spirit wants to do is to magnify, lift up, exalt, and glorify Jesus.

This is a responsibility of the Holy Spirit that is always grand and glorious and totally pleasurable to believers who allow Him to move this way in their walk with God. Worshiping the Lord in communion with the Holy Spirit is what makes Jesus Christ real in the believer's daily life. Nothing else so deeply and completely fulfills and satisfies the spirit and soul of man.

Think About It

It is the Holy Spirit's greatest joy to make Jesus real to you and to reveal to you more and more of Jesus' nature, thoughts, and desires concerning you and His plan and purpose for your life. Worship is key to the Holy Spirit's work of revealing a deeper understanding of Christ. How can you cultivate an atmosphere of continual worship in your daily life that makes it easy for the Spirit of God to carry out this revealing work to His fullest capacity?

CHAPTER FOURTEEN

THE JEALOUSY
OF THE HOLY SPIRIT

> **Ye adulterers and adulteresses, know ye not that friendship of the world is enmity with God? Whosoever therefore will be a friend of the world is the enemy of God. Do ye think that the scripture saith in vain, The spirit that dwelleth in us lusteth to envy?"**
>
> **— James 4:4,5**

Since we are studying how to develop a more intimate and personal relationship with the Holy Spirit, these verses in James 4 are particularly important for us. In them, James — inspired by the Holy Spirit Himself — actually leveled the charge of adultery against a group of believers!

This is an especially strong accusation when you consider that he was writing to moral Jewish believers. Even before they became Christians, they would never have dreamed of committing adultery. Adulterers and adulteresses were stoned to death under Jewish law.

James couldn't have said anything more shocking, hurtful, or outrageous to these believers in Jesus Christ! For a Jew, nothing was more insulting than this. But since they were moral people who would never actually commit adultery, why *did* James call them adulterers and adulteresses? The answer lies in what James asked next: "...Know ye not that the friendship of the world is enmity with God?..."

These believers had been drawn into an improper relationship with the world. To get their attention and drive this very serious point into their hearts, James called them *adulterers* and *adulteresses.*

The *King James Version* mentions both "adulterers and adulteresses." But the Greek version of the New Testament simply says *"ye adulteresses."* Later in this chapter, I'll tell you why this is important.

The word "adultery" has all kinds of connotations, such as *unfaithfulness, impurity,* and *the violation of a commitment to marriage,* to name just a few. We normally associate adultery with a spouse who has engaged in a sexual relationship outside of his or her marriage. When this betrayal of the marriage covenant is discovered, the violated spouse feels such deep hurt that nothing else in the world can be compared to it.

Even the death of a spouse can be less difficult to process than the betrayal of a spouse who has committed adultery. Feelings of rejection and the hurt of being lied to, misled, and deceived can threaten to emotionally consume a person in that situation. These are just some of the terribly strong and painful emotions the spouse feels when the sanctity and security of the marriage relationship has been recklessly thrown away by the adulterer or adulteress.

When Denise and I were first married, we were the ministers for the single adults in a large Southern Baptist church. We developed a program to help those who were newly divorced. We learned that most of these people felt like they were outcasts from the Church. When we opened our hearts to minister to them and made "life after divorce" a well-known emphasis of our ministry, newly divorced people came to us from all over that region.

In one year's time, we ministered to approximately 800 people who had been through a divorce. It was one of the most gratifying, yet troublesome periods of ministry we have ever experienced. It was gratifying to see people who had been so rejected and wounded being healed by the love of Jesus Christ. But it was difficult for Denise and me to so often hear the outpouring of agonizing emotions that these precious people went through as a result of being betrayed by someone they trusted.

Day after day, we'd sit and listen as each one told us his or her story. Out of hundreds of cases, more than two-thirds of them sounded identical — so identical that if I had wanted to, I could eventually finish most of their stories before they were done telling them.

Again and again, these dear, emotionally broken people said things like, "I just don't know how he could do that to me! After all these years of being faithful to him, raising our children with him, and working to help him through school — *how could he do this to me?* I gave my life to him the best I knew how. How could he dump me and go after someone else?"

Or we heard, "How could she do this to me after I've given her so much? I gave her my love, my attention — I gave all that I knew to give! *How could she do this!*"

In nearly every session, Denise and I would hear people trying to express their raw emotions. Over and over we would hear things like, "I feel as if my heart has been ripped out and stomped on!" Or we heard, "I feel like I've been kicked in the gut and have had the wind knocked out of me."

We came to conclude that betrayal by a spouse is possibly the worst betrayal of all in the human experience. Nothing seems to hurt worse, cut deeper, or last longer than this type of emotional trauma.

Earlier I said I would explain why the Greek just says "adulteresses" instead of "adulterers and adulteresses." James wrote his book for the members of the Church, which is the Bride of Christ. In some way that James doesn't describe, this group of believers had gone outside their relationship with Christ to find fulfillment and companionship with someone or something else. Therefore, they'd been unfaithful to their "Spouse," Jesus Christ, and had become adulteresses.

Sin affects not only us individually, but also the indwelling Holy Spirit. He actually feels hurt and grief, as of a violated spouse. When this truth becomes revelation to our hearts, it will change our permissive attitude toward sin and cause us to live more consecrated lives for Jesus Christ.

James called these good, moral Jewish believers "adulteresses" because they went outside their marriage to Christ to find fulfillment. They were giving their minds, hearts, and lives to worldly things. They had committed spiritual adultery.

What Is Friendship With the World?

The word "friendship" is from the word *phileo*. This word carries the idea of an intense fondness that is developed between people who enjoy each other's company. It describes love between family members as well as other human relationships. It speaks of two or more people who know one another, who are fond of one another, and who are growing more deeply involved in each other's lives.

Usually the word *phileo* conveys the idea of *a friend with whom you desire to have a deeper relationship*. In a certain sense, this attraction is so great that it leads to being preoccupied with someone or something. It involves giving your attention, your time, your devotion, and your love to that person. That is what friendship demands if it is a relationship to be maintained through the years.

That is precisely the condition James was talking about when he said, "The friendship of the world is enmity with God" (James 4:4). He wasn't judging these believers for having expensive tastes, working at good jobs, desiring nice houses, or driving beautiful cars. The phrase "friendship of the world" was not about owning things; rather, it was about being *consumed* or *preoccupied* with the things of this world.

Those to whom James wrote his epistle were getting tangled up in the thinking, the behavior, and the material possessions of the world. One reason we know they were struggling with this tendency to worldliness is found in the previous verses. There James said their prayers weren't being answered because they were asking God for things with wrong motives. Rather than desiring things so they could help others, they selfishly wanted more and more things for themselves. James told them, "Ye ask, and receive not, because ye ask amiss, that ye may consume it upon your lusts" (James 4:3).

These people were Jewish believers who had always lived holy lives — but at the time of this writing, it appears that these believers were being seduced by the things of the world. This process of seduction had progressed to the point of their being *attracted to, consumed with*, and *preoccupied with* the world. This attraction had already become so great that they had entered into friendship with the world. They had gone outside of their relationship with Christ to give their hearts and minds to something else. *They had committed spiritual adultery.*

James wasn't teaching that having nice possessions is wrong. Rather, he was telling us that it is wrong to be so consumed and preoccupied with the things of the world that we don't have time or the desire to think of anything else.

Flirting with the world will eventually lead to an ungodly connection with the things of the world. It is spiritual adultery toward the Lord Jesus Christ to be so involved with the current status quo of society that you begin to think as they do, act as they do, and seek the same things they do. Having material possessions, social status, and so forth, in your hand is one thing — but having these things in your *heart* is another. When the things of the world get in your heart and you become preoccupied with them, you have crossed a serious line.

TALKING YOURSELF INTO SIN

James went on to say in verse 4, "…Whosoever therefore will be a friend of the world…." I especially want you to notice the words "will be" in this phrase. They are taken from the Greek word *boulomai*, which means *to counsel* or *to resolve*.

> **When the things of the world get in your heart and you become preoccupied with them, you have crossed a serious line.**

This word *boulomai* could describe *a counseling session* or *seeking the counsel of someone else*. As it is used in this verse, the word *boulomai* doesn't describe some other counselor listening to you and advising you. This time the counselor is *you*! You are counseling yourself.

This presents a snapshot of a Christian who is being seduced by the world. Rather than saying a firm *no* to ungodliness, as Titus 2:12 instructs, he chooses to draw nearer to the world for a closer look. In essence, it is this "flirting" with sin that eventually leads to the practice of it.

This Christian feels his flesh being lured by the world. Sensing the warning of the Holy Spirit to withdraw from the situation and walk in holiness, he turns a deaf ear to the Spirit in order to listen to his flesh. Before this person knows it, he is talking himself into doing what he knows is wrong. He may think to himself: *Well, I know I shouldn't, but just a little won't hurt.... I know it will probably grieve the Holy Spirit, but God will forgive me.... I can't believe I'm doing this, and I know I shouldn't. But I'm going to do it just this time....*

This Christian literally talks (in other words, "counsels") himself into doing what he knows is wrong. This is the process of sin in the soul. It is seductive and deceptive. It tries to lure the soul to lay aside godly convictions and to follow the dictates of the flesh to indulge in carnal pleasures that last only for a moment.

THE TEMPTATION OF WORLDLINESS

James was speaking to Christians who had counseled themselves into doing what they would never have dreamed of doing before. In essence, he was saying, *"If you've become the friend of the world, here's the reason: You've made so many little exceptions for yourself that now what used to bother you doesn't bother you at all. In fact, over a period of time, you've become a worldly Christian with worldly thinking and worldly behavior!"*

Worldliness tries to wrap its arms around all of us. Not one of us is exempt from its seductive pull.

Take a moment to honestly evaluate yourself. Just think of the things you tolerate in your life today that you would never have tolerated ten years ago.

- *Do you watch television programs or movies today that you would have considered a sin ten years ago?*

- *Are you more permissive in your thinking about sin today than you used to be?*

- *Are there any areas of your life that used to be more on fire and less compromising than they are right now?*

- *Do you pray and witness as much as you once did?*

You might as well be honest with God because He knows your real spiritual condition anyway. You can't bluff Him by saying, "Well, here's the reason I didn't obey You. I would have done what You said, but..." If the Holy Spirit has pointed out an area of your life in which you are worldly, just agree with Him and say, "Yes, Lord, I see that I've been worldly in that area. Please forgive me and help me change. As an act of my obedience and faith, I willingly commit myself to You and Your Word so that genuine change can occur."

> Worldliness tries to wrap its arms around all of us. Not one of us is exempt from its seductive pull.

Getting honest with God will position you correctly so He can then work in your heart and help you. Once you recognize your guilt and admit it, you're back to being honest with God, and you can grow again.

We could all admit a tendency toward worldliness in some area of our lives. But if we don't deal with these areas as the Holy Spirit leads us, over time we will become more conformed to the world than to Jesus Christ.

Being a friend to the world doesn't happen overnight. It takes time. Very slowly, seductively, and methodically, our thinking, our behavior, and our outlook on life can grow to look more and more similar to that of the world than to that of Jesus.

This is what James meant when he said, "Whosoever therefore *will be* a friend of the world...." Those words "will be" are very important for you and me. They indicate that our sin is *our* responsibility. We cannot blame our behavior on our environment, on our friends, or on anything else.

> If we lose the spiritual fire that is intended to continually burn in our hearts, we can know that we've counseled ourselves into believing that sin is acceptable when it's not.

If we lose the spiritual fire that is intended to continually burn in our hearts, we can know that we've counseled ourselves into believing that sin is acceptable when it's not. We are living out the result of our own self-deceived conclusion.

Think About It

Often we define "worldliness" by the obvious vices we know we are to avoid as Christians. But the spirit of the world can act like a spiritual "carbon monoxide" — toxic, invisible fumes that permeate the atmosphere and poison the unaware. Through various forms of media, conversations with other people, and so forth, our ears will invariably hear words every day that are contrary to what God says. Those words often carry the power of death that eventually infiltrates our souls through the slow creep of compromise.

Take some time to evaluate how you've been doing as the watchman at the "gates" of your own life — your eyes, your ears, and your mouth. You are the one who decides what comes in and goes out. Have you been faithful at your post? Are you quick to say, "Illegal entry — no trespassing!" to anything that would draw you into friendship with the world at the expense of your fellowship with the precious Holy Spirit?

CHAPTER FIFTEEN

THE HOLY SPIRIT CAN BE GRIEVED

*E*phesians 4:30 tells us how all those little exceptions we make when we "counsel" ourselves into sin affect the Holy Spirit: "And grieve not the holy Spirit of God, whereby ye are sealed unto the day of redemption." If we want to develop intimate communion with the Holy Spirit, the last thing we want to do is grieve Him.

The word "grieve" comes from the Greek word *lupete*. This was a very special word. It was used to denote *the emotions of a betrayed spouse*, similar to the emotions I described in the previous chapter. Feeling betrayed, deceived, lied to, misled, hurt, wounded, and abused — all of these vividly portray the emotions of a spouse who has discovered that his or her mate has been unfaithful.

Now we find that the word *lupete* is used by Paul in Ephesians 4:30 to describe how we affect the indwelling Holy Spirit when we tend toward worldliness. Paul leaves no doubt regarding what he is telling us. When we cease to make our relationship with the Holy Spirit the number-one priority in our lives and allow other things to take His rightful place, it hurts Him the same way it hurts a spouse to learn that his or her mate has been unfaithful.

Jesus is Lord, but the Holy Spirit is the One who lives in us, leads us, guides us, teaches us, reminds us, comforts us, seals us, sanctifies us, empowers us, and works to produce the character of Christ in us. The Spirit of God has been sent to reveal the will of God, which is the mind of Christ, and to cause us to walk in the victory that Jesus won through His death and resurrection.

> The Holy Spirit is here for *us*. That is why He was sent. Therefore, when we ignore Him, turn a deaf ear to Him, or consistently disobey what He nudges us to do, it grieves Him.

The Holy Spirit is here for *us*. That is why He was sent. Therefore, when we ignore Him, turn a deaf ear to Him, or consistently disobey what He nudges us to do, it grieves Him.

But let's be even more specific about what grieves the Holy Spirit. In the verses surrounding Ephesians 4:30, Paul gave the following examples:

- Lying (v. 25)

- Letting the sun go down on your wrath (v. 26)

- Giving place to the devil (v. 27)

- Stealing (v. 28)

- Letting corrupt communication proceed out of your mouth (v. 29)

- Not putting away all bitterness, wrath, anger, clamor, evil speaking, and malice (v. 31)

All of these are fleshly acts that grieve the Holy Spirit. And it's important to remember that Paul was speaking to Christians when he wrote those verses. Unfortunately, that means Christians were committing these sins! These "temples of the Holy Spirit" were lying, holding on to grudges and anger, giving place to the devil, stealing, talking evil to and about one another, giving bitterness a place in their hearts, and allowing themselves to be angry and to hold malice against each other.

No wonder the Holy Spirit was grieved! He had come to produce holiness in the Ephesian believers, but worldliness was dominating their lives, and they were quenching Him. He was being left out of the picture, much like a spouse who has been betrayed.

The fact that Paul used the word "grieve" tells us the Holy Spirit felt wounded by the wrong behavior and attitudes of certain believers in the Ephesian church. He felt like a spouse who was being dragged through the mud by an unfaithful mate. After all He had done within these believers to help them grow and become more like Jesus, how could they now push the Holy Spirit aside and give in to their flesh in such a manner?

We need to think before we talk and act. We need to remember that Someone lives inside us whose name is the Holy Spirit. The reason He is called the Holy Spirit is that He is holy. Romans 1:4 calls Him "the spirit of holiness." That is who He is, and that is what He comes to produce in our lives.

You would never think of throwing mud and garbage all over a beautiful cathedral. Your conscience couldn't bear the guilt of knowing you had personally desecrated a finely decorated church building. Yet *you* are of far more worth than that cathedral! The Holy Spirit doesn't live in buildings; He lives in *you*.

In spite of this, we throw mud and garbage into our lives all the time, not thinking of how it must grieve the Spirit of holiness who lives inside us. We drag Him through the mud of our lives every time we sin — especially when we do it deliberately.

Of course, this grief the Holy Spirit experiences when we sin doesn't preclude His tenderness when we repent for our wrong behavior. The Holy Spirit comes quickly to our aid when we're truly repentant to restore us to our place of intimate fellowship with the Lord.

According to Ephesians 4, the sins that Christians find most difficult to resist aren't usually the more obvious sins such as drunkenness or sexual impurity. The sins we must deal with most often are wrong inner attitudes that we can all tend to harbor, such as unforgiveness, bitterness, resentment, anger, or malice. We shouldn't allow these attitudes to remain in us, if for no other reason than we know they grieve the Holy Spirit. But besides that, such attitudes can also give the enemy a foothold to gain access into our lives, leaving us more susceptible to temptation by those "external" sins just mentioned (*see* Hebrews 12:15,16).

The next time you're tempted to hold resentment in your heart toward someone, ask yourself the question, *If I harbor this attitude, will it grieve the Holy Spirit in my life?*

If we simply make ourselves more aware of the Holy Spirit's indwelling presence, it will help change the way we think and live. It will most definitely help us think before we talk and act.

Remember, the Holy Spirit lives inside you. What you do in your life today, you do to Him as well. Where you go today, you take Him with you. If you go to a questionable movie, He goes with you. If you choose to sin, you are dragging Him with you through that grievous act.

Do you really want to grieve the Holy Spirit? Of course not! The Holy Spirit lives in you and deserves your utmost reverence and respect.

CAN A CHRISTIAN BECOME AN ENEMY OF GOD?

Living as a worldly Christian is serious business! That's why James 4:4 says, *"A friend of the world is the enemy of God."*

Notice the word "is." It's the Greek word *kathistemi*, which means *to constitute* or *to render.* Christians who choose to take a worldly path have set themselves in opposition to the godly path God desires for them. As a result of their own choice, they have *rendered* or *constituted* themselves to be the enemies of God.

The word "enemy" in James 4:4 comes from the Greek word *echthros*, which describes an extremely opposite attitude to love and friendship. Whereas love and friendship mean warmth, commitment, and relationship, the word *echthros* means *extreme hostility, intense disrespect,* and *an all-consuming hatred.*

James was telling us: "If you choose warmth and friendship with the world, this will put you in direct opposition to God." That is *not* a good place to be.

Romans 8:31 declares, "...If God be for us, who can be against us?" By the same token, *if God is against us, who can be for us?* If God is against us, we are "finished" in our own pursuits, and we can count on the fact that frustration lies in our future.

However, if we choose friendship with God, we position ourselves in direct opposition to the friendship of the world. This opposition is so strong that it makes us enemies with the world. And remember, the word "enemy" carries the idea of *hatred.* In other words, the world — its system and ways of thinking and behaving — hates us for our friendship with God.

Jesus used the word "hate" when He said, "No man can serve two masters: for either he will hate the one, and love the other; or else he will hold to the one, and despise the other. Ye cannot serve God and mammon" (Matthew 6:24).

According to Jesus, it is impossible for us as Christians to give our hearts simultaneously to two masters. We must choose whom we are going to serve: *God* or *mammon*. Mammon was an expression used by the Jewish community of that time to express the idea of *worldliness*.

The word "serve" comes from the word *doulos*. It is where we get the word for *a servant* or *a slave*. This word was used to denote *a servant who had given himself over entirely to another person or thing*. This person was a slave for a lifetime.

This slave *serviced* something or someone with almost all of his attention, time, and energy. In other words, this slave catered to his master's every wish, desire, or demand. He was there to help, assist, and fulfill his master's wants and needs and had no time for anything else.

When you buy a car, washing machine, or even a house, it must be serviced to keep it in working order. These things will operate for a while without your attention, but in time you must give your attention to them in order to keep them in good running condition. If you own a house, you know a house requires all kinds of time, attention, energy, and money.

Similarly, if you want your spiritual walk with God to remain in good working order, it won't happen accidentally. It's going to take effort and time.

When Jesus said, "Ye cannot serve God and mammon," He was giving us this very important truth. Both God and mammon are going to require a wholehearted investment of your time, attention, energy, and money. There is not enough of you to service both God and worldliness in your life. Hence, you must choose which you will serve.

Serving God means spending time with Him, learning to know His voice, and developing a pattern of obedience in your daily walk. It will require you to serve God with your entire life for all of your days — even as you're attending to your family, your job or career, and the everyday affairs of life. Living for God will demand your fullest attention. A life lived for Him must be serviced continually with prayer, obedience, repentance, and worship.

Here's the good news: Jesus promised that if we would seek Him first, He would make certain that everything we needed in a material way would be added to us (*see* Matthew 6:33). *That* is supernatural living!

> **Living for God will demand your fullest attention. A life lived for Him must be serviced continually with prayer, obedience, repentance, and worship.**

Serving mammon (the world) means giving your fullest attention to material pursuits. If you're going to be successful according to the world's standards, you won't have room for anything else in your life. You certainly won't have time for reading the Word of God, praying, and setting aside time just to worship and wait before the Lord. Serving mammon will require all of your time, attention, energy, and money.

That is why Jesus said we must hold to and love one master, and we must hate and despise the other. And should we ever fall into the trap of loving the wrong master for a season, we need to repent — *change* — and begin serving Jesus wholeheartedly once again!

WHOM DO *YOU* SERVE?

Let me ask you this question: What are you serving in your life right now? What most requires your time and attention? Can you truthfully say you are giving God your fullest attention and that the chief priority in your life is to serve and obey Him? Or must you admit that worldly pursuits, possessions, and corporate success consume too much of your attention and energies?

If you're consumed with God, these other things have a lower place on your list of priorities than He does. But if you're consumed with the friendship of the world, material things will dominate the landscape of your mind.

Just stop and ask yourself, *What do I think about more than anything else in life?* Your answer will probably tell you whom you are serving with your time and talents.

God will stand in opposition to the Christian who is outside the life He has planned for him or her. That is why James 4:6 says, "...God resisteth the proud...."

> **Just stop and ask yourself, *What do I think about more than anything else in life?* Your answer will probably tell you whom you are serving with your time and talents.**

The word "resisteth" is the Greek word *antisteste* from *anthistemi*, and it means *to stand against, to oppose,* or *to take a stand against another.* A believer who has chosen to go his own way has chosen to take a stand against God. If this believer doesn't repent and come back to where God wants him to be, God will oppose him and take a stand against *him.* That Christian can rebuke the devil's power all day long, but it will be to no avail. That person's problem is not the devil. His problem is that he has turned his back on God and the plan of God for his life.

I can't imagine anything worse than a Christian who is being opposed by God. Things just don't seem to work right or turn out the way they should. The path of worldliness is a hard road for a believer to take.

If God is standing against us, our plans will fail, our dreams will come to naught, and nothing in life will succeed. Frustration, worry, anxiety, and feelings of failure are just a few of the negative emotions we will experience if God is blocking our way.

This resistance from God, as terrible as it may sound, is an act of His grace. By blocking our ways and resisting our choices, God's precious Holy Spirit endeavors to bring us to a place of sweet brokenness where sin is confessed and fellowship with Him is restored.

Think About It

From the moment you received Jesus as your Lord and Savior and the Holy Spirit moved in as the permanent Resident of your spirit man, He has been your constant Companion. He has been an intimate witness of your every action, word, and thought. The more aware you are of the Holy Spirit's continual presence in your life, the more your desire will grow to never grieve Him — and the easier it will become for you to yield to His promptings and recognize what He is saying to you in your heart.

What can you do to cultivate a growing awareness of the Holy Spirit's presence within you? How can you effectively tap into His assistance that is continually available to you in every area of your life?

CHAPTER SIXTEEN

A PERMANENT INDWELLER

"*D*o ye think that the scripture saith in vain, The spirit that dwelleth in us lusteth to envy?" (James 4:5). This verse explains why God reacts so strongly to Christians who get wrapped up in worldliness instead of the Holy Spirit.

I am convinced that it is a lack of understanding that permits believers to do the wrong things they do. If they were intimately acquainted with the One who lives inside them and truly understood His holy nature, they wouldn't be able to tolerate hurting or grieving Him. That's why we need more teaching on the Person and work of the Holy Spirit!

Understanding the internal work of the Holy Spirit in our lives is central to our being saved, sanctified, and empowered for daily service. How do we think we can proceed in the power of God without this basic foundation in place? This foundational knowledge is not optional — it is a *necessity*.

In light of this truth of the Holy Spirit's indwelling presence, let's look at what James meant when he wrote, "Do ye think the scripture saith in vain, The spirit that dwelleth in us lusteth to envy?"

There are three key words that we must consider in this verse: 1) "dwelleth," 2) "lusteth," and 3) "envy." First, let's look at the word "dwelleth." In Chapter Ten, we saw that the Holy Spirit comes to live in us at our new birth. He doesn't just come for a visit — He comes to be a *permanent Indweller.*

> **Understanding the internal work of the Holy Spirit in our lives is central to our being saved, sanctified, and empowered for daily service. This foundational knowledge is not optional — it is a *necessity.***

The word "dwelleth" used in John 14:17, which we discussed earlier, is *meno*, which means *to permanently abide or dwell.* But in James 4:5, the word *dwelleth* is taken from the Greek word *katoikizo.* This word is a compound of the words *kata* and *oikos.* The word *kata* means *according to,* and *oikos* is the Greek word for *a house.* When compounded, the new word means *to take up residency* or *to dwell in a house.*

This word carries the idea of *residing permanently.* In other words, this word would never describe a transient or one who came only to live temporarily in a place. This Greek word paints the picture of a person who was born and raised and who had married, worked, had children, retired, died, and been buried *all in the same city.* This person had never wanted to move away and live anywhere else. That place had been his home, and he'd wanted it to remain his home for his entire life.

In other words, when the Holy Spirit came to live in you, it wasn't for a short period of time. He came to *stay.* From that point onward, He made your heart His home. He has, so to speak, hung His own pictures on the walls of your heart, laid His own rugs on the floor, moved His furniture in, and settled down into a nice, big, comfortable chair. He has no intention of ever leaving to live somewhere else.

The Holy Spirit has come to be a permanent Indweller in your heart. Your heart is not a hotel to which He comes to visit occasionally. Your heart is His home. He is the One who lives inside you and never leaves.

A Cathedral for the Spirit

In a figure of speech, I have said the Holy Spirit has hung pictures on the wall of your heart, put rugs on the floor, and settled into a comfortable chair. But He has done so much more. In the new birth, He has taken our spirits, which were dead in trespasses and sin, and raised them to new life, recreating them to become the marvelous temple of God.

Obviously, what the Holy Spirit accomplished in your salvation was not just a *decorating* job. He created a dwelling place inside you so wonderful, so marvelous, and so outstanding that God Himself — in the Person of the Holy Spirit — was willing to make it His home.

Paul referred to this miraculous work when he wrote, "What? Know ye not that your body is the temple of the Holy Ghost which is in you, which ye have of God, and ye are not your own? For ye are bought with a price: therefore glorify God in your body, and in your spirit, which are God's" (1 Corinthians 6:19,20).

The word "temple" in this passage is taken from the word *naos*, which always describes *a highly decorated shrine*. The word "shrine" paints a picture of a beautiful cathedral that has tall, vaulted ceilings, marble columns, granite floors, hand-carved woodwork overlaid with gold and silver, crystal chandeliers, silver candelabras, and burning incense around the front of the altar.

Being raised a Southern Baptist, I was accustomed to the interior of a Baptist church. We had pews, a baptistry, nice carpet, and heavy oak pulpit furniture. That was our style of church decoration. It was nice, but moderate and simple.

The first time I entered a cathedral, I nearly fell over. I was just a small boy when I participated in my uncle's wedding at a large Catholic church in our city. I remember walking down the aisle of that church building, simply awestruck by the height of the ceilings and the beauty of the statues and paintings.

In my journeys from one end of the former Soviet Union to the other, I often stop to see the large Russian Orthodox church buildings that cover the land. The craftsmanship of the architecture, the inlaid marble, the paintings, the icons, and the gold, silver, and precious stones — everything I see is so beautiful that I can't even imagine the level of talent required to create them. Some of these buildings are nearly unbelievable in terms of size, beauty, and intensity of splendor. To say they are spectacular is downplaying their beauty. This is precisely what Paul meant when he said that we are *temples* of the Holy Spirit.

It is warm and cozy to think of the Holy Spirit making Himself at home in our spiritual houses. I personally appreciate meditating on the sense of permanence that comes from knowing that the Holy Spirit makes Himself at home inside us. But because Paul used the word *naos* ("temple") in First Corinthians 6:19 to describe us, he was painting a very different picture than that of a warm and cozy house.

The Holy Spirit did the ultimate miracle when He came to dwell in our hearts. He took our spirits, which were dead in trespasses and sin (*see* Ephesians 2:1), and He quickened us together with Christ (*see* Ephesians 2:5). In that miraculous moment, He created our spirits to be like God in righteousness and true holiness (*see* Ephesians 4:24).

This work inside us was so glorious and perfect that when it was all finished, the Father declared that we were His workmanship, created in Christ Jesus (*see* Ephesians 2:10). From start to finish, we were apprehended by Him, regenerated by Him, and molded and fashioned by Him to be the temple of the Spirit of God.

This makes salvation the greatest miracle of all. The change in our previously dead spiritual nature is truly miraculous. The Father resurrected our nature and filled it with glory, power, revelation, holiness, splendor, righteousness, the fruit of the Spirit, the gifts of the Spirit, and the life and character of Christ. He lavishly adorned our inner man until, spiritually speaking, we became a priceless shrine to the glory of God.

Inwardly we are so beautiful and magnificently created that Almighty God, through His Spirit, is willing to take up permanent residency within us. What kind of home do you think God would require? A shabby shack made of dirt and sticks? No! He has built for Himself an exquisite temple within our hearts.

> The Father resurrected our nature and filled it with glory, power, revelation, holiness, splendor, righteousness, the fruit of the Spirit, the gifts of the Spirit, and the life and character of Christ. He lavishly adorned our inner man until, spiritually speaking, we became a priceless shrine to the glory of God.

WHAT YOU SEE IS NOT WHAT YOU GET!

Many of us have poor self-images. We see ourselves as unworthy shacks built of mud and sticks. We certainly do not see ourselves as highly decorated shrines of the Holy Spirit. And, naturally speaking, we *are* fairly weak as human beings.

Paul was aware of this too. That's why he wrote, "But we have this treasure in earthen vessels, that the excellency of the power may be of God, and not of us" (2 Corinthians 4:7).

Paul used several key words in this text. First, he said, "But we have...." The Greek word used here for "we have" is *echomen*, and it can also be translated "we hold" or "we possess." It is in agreement with the phrase "earthen vessels," which is the Greek word *ostrakinos*, describing *small, cheap, easily broken pottery*. This particular kind of pottery was considered to be weak, fragile, and of minimal value.

By using the word *echomen* in connection with the *ostrakinos*, Paul was making a strong statement regarding our real spiritual condition. He stated that we *hold, contain*, or *possess* some kind of treasure in vessels that are small, cheap, easily broken, and without any real value. That is how he described our physical bodies.

Paul was right. The human body is fragile. A wrong diet can kill it; working too hard can break it; too much pressure can damage it. And even after caring tenderly for it our whole lifetime, it still dies.

The greatest minds, the most creative inventors, the highest intellects, the most colorful writers, and the most talented politicians all die. Eventually the human body breaks under the stress of age, and the vessel that carried such incredible talent and potential is reduced to unrecognizable dust, totally devoid of value. Some human vessels break earlier and some last longer, but eventually they all break, they all collapse, and they all return to dust.

Here is the amazing part: These "earthen vessels" of ours contain or hold something Paul called a *treasure*. The word "treasure" is the word *thesauros*. It describes *a treasure so rich and so immense that it could never be expended.* This would be the treasure hunter's greatest dream, because we've also been given the treasure map! As always, "X" marks the spot for hidden treasure, and this time the Bible has written the "X" on us. *We are God's hiding place for secret treasure.*

From natural appearances, we may look weak, fragile, and devoid of true value. Certainly we do not look like a place where God would hide His greatest treasure. Yet Paul wrote this verse, almost with a sense of amazement: *"We hold this immense, incredibly rich, inexhaustible treasure in these human bodies of ours that are so easily broken and expended!"*

If you were God and had a treasure so infinitely grand, would *you* place it in something as unreliable as your physical body? You would probably have to say no. But that is what God did — and *that* is part of the miracle of salvation.

What we see with our natural eyes is a display of weak humanity. But contained in our fleshly, carnal, short-lived body is the very power that created the universe and raised Jesus from the dead!

The Holy Spirit recreated us in Christ Jesus, turning our previously dead spirits into temples so marvelous that He is willing to dwell there permanently as God's greatest treasure given to mankind. The Holy Spirit has put all of His energies and invested all of Heaven's riches into us to make a dwelling place worthy for God Himself. He called us, sealed us, sanctified us, and filled us with His holiness. Inside our human spirit, we are the highly decorated shrine of Almighty God.

> **Contained in our fleshly, carnal, short-lived body is the very power that created the universe and raised Jesus from the dead!**

So after all of that divine effort born out of unconditional love, do you think the Holy Spirit is going to just walk off and leave His investment? I assure you that He won't!

That is why Paul went on to admonish the Corinthian believers by saying, "For ye are bought with a price: therefore glorify God in your body...and spirit" (1 Corinthians 6:20). In the oldest Greek versions of this verse, Paul admonished them to glorify God in *the body* rather than in the body *and* the spirit. That's because the body is the issue in this verse, not the spirit of man.

Our spirit man is inhabited by the Holy Spirit. Our problem is not with our human spirit, where the Holy Spirit dwells. Our issue concerns what we do with our *body*, which houses our recreated human spirit. We engage in a dreadful hypocrisy when we serve as the temple of the Holy Spirit who dwells inside us and adorns us inwardly with His glory and power — yet outwardly we mingle and mix with the world through our physical senses and our thought life.

> We engage in a dreadful hypocrisy when we serve as the temple of the Holy Spirit who dwells inside us and adorns us inwardly with His glory and power — yet outwardly we mingle and mix with the world through our physical senses and our thought life.

When Paul wrote the Corinthian believers about gluttony, sexual immorality, and worldliness, he told them, "Know ye not that your bodies are the members of Christ? Shall I then take the members of Christ, and make them the members of an harlot? God forbid. What? Know ye not that he which is joined to an harlot is one body? For two, saith he, shall be one flesh. But he that is joined unto the Lord is one spirit" (1 Corinthians 6:15-17). Then he concluded with the statement that we've been examining: "…Therefore glorify God in your body…" (v. 20).

Verse 20 articulates the purpose that is to motivate every thought, every word, and every action in your walk with God on this earth: *You are to glorify Him.*

You see, once you gave your life to Jesus Christ and asked Him to be the Lord of your life, He did what you asked. He sent His Spirit to create you anew and to live in your heart. Now you are not your own. Paul said that you were "*bought* with a price." Jesus purchased you with His own precious blood. Now — spirit, soul, and body — you are *His.*

This is why it is so grievous to the Holy Spirit when we walk back into the world or pick up a worldly attitude that begins to govern our thoughts, words, and actions. We drag Him right into the middle of an unholy situation, and we become offensive to the holiness of God. Whenever we mingle our bodies and minds with the world, Paul says it is the same as taking the members of Christ and uniting them to a harlot.

Imagine a wife saying to her husband, "I love you, and I want to stay married to you forever. But I have authority over my own body, will, and emotions, and I want to have an affair with another man." To believers in Jesus Christ, such an attitude is completely unacceptable! How dare a wife violate her marriage vows in such a detestable manner and defile her covenant with her husband! And the same is true if the spouse with the unholy attitude is the husband!

But that is too frequently what believers do to the Lord Jesus Christ. They declare their vow of surrender and obedience to Him at the moment they call Him Lord. Then at some point in their walk with Jesus, they violate their covenant with Him by reuniting themselves with the spirit of the world.

What about you? The Holy Spirit goes where you go and sees what you see. Are you taking Him to places that He would never lead you?

When we understand that the Holy Spirit lives in us, it will change the way we perceive ourselves and the way we do business in life. It will change the way we think, talk, and behave.

What an honor to be the dwelling place of the Holy Spirit! Just stop and think about it one more time — Almighty God designed for Himself a home in your heart! What greater honor is there than this? If you need a self-image booster, stop and meditate on that fact. *All the riches and treasures of Jesus Christ permanently reside within you* (*see* Colossians 2:3).

We must remember that we are members of Christ and that what we do to ourselves, we do to Him as well. He indwells us through the Person of the Holy Spirit. We *must* learn to honor and respect the presence of God in our lives.

Think About It

You are a carrier of the Holy Spirit's presence, and your primary assignment in this life is to learn to yield to His leading in every situation. Wherever you go, you take the treasure of His glory, and He desires to manifest that glory *through* you.

Take the time to revisit your past week. Sift through the whole range of motives that caused you to do what you did and say what you said. If there were any wrong motives, repent and discard them. Then assess the things you said and did with the *right* motives and notice the connecting thread through it all — *to glorify Jesus.* Wherever you find that pure desire to glorify God, nurture it by pressing deeper in your fellowship with the Holy Spirit. He is the Originator of that heart's desire, as well as the Facilitator who ensures its fulfillment.

CHAPTER SEVENTEEN

THE DIVINE LOVER

*I*n the last chapter, we looked at the word "dwelleth" in James 4:5: "…The Spirit that dwelleth in us lusteth to envy." The next word we must consider is the word "lusteth."

For the most part, the word "lust" has a very bad connotation in our minds. We think of it as sexual lust, for example — something that must be eradicated from our lives. We think of a greedy form of lust, such as an excessive desire for material possessions. Lust is something we don't want to confess proudly as a part of our lives. We want to get rid of it.

But James wrote that the Holy Spirit has a type of lust! Because He is the Spirit of holiness (*see* Romans 1:4), the lust of the Holy Spirit must be a *healthy, godly* kind of lust. This point about the lust of the Holy Spirit is so important that we must stop and see exactly what James is saying to us here.

The word "lusteth" is taken from the Greek word *epipothei*, which is a compound of two Greek words, *epi* and *pothei*. The word *epi* means "for," and the word *pothei* means *an intense desire or yearning*.

When these two words are compounded as we find them in James 4:5, the new word describes *an intense, beyond-normal, excessive yearning.* Usually this word is used to indicate something that is morally wrong or sinful.

For example, this word could adequately be used to picture a drug addict. Every day the addict needs a new fix of drugs to carry him into the next day. When the last fix wears off, and his body is desperately crying out for a new infusion of chemicals, he is nearly doubled over in pain — yearning, straining, and crying out for the next "fix." Everything in him is focused on getting those chemicals. He is consumed with his need for more. The word *epipothei* could describe that kind of yearning.

Why would James use this word to describe the Holy Spirit? Does the Holy Spirit really have lust? Yes, but this is a positive kind of lust! The Greek word for "lust" in this verse could read, *"The Spirit that dwelleth in us has an intense, excessive, beyond-the-normal yearning...."* So what does this verse mean? What is the Holy Spirit yearning for so passionately? What does the Holy Spirit desire to possess so intensely?

You Are the Object of the Holy Spirit's Love and Affection

After all the Holy Spirit has done in us, it should be no great shock to discover the Holy Spirit is in love with us. The fact that He views our mixing and mingling with the world as adultery should alert us to the intense love and affection He has for us.

The Holy Spirit was sent to be our Helper and Comforter. Although He does many other things, His primary job is to help us receive Jesus Christ, help us grow as Christians, help us witness, help us worship, help us understand God's Word, and so on.

The Holy Spirit is our Indweller, our Sealer, our Sanctifier, our Power, and the Source of our new life in Christ. His work, His attention, His gifts, His power, and His Word are all directed toward us. We are the object of His love and affection.

As a divine Lover who lives on the inside of us, the Holy Spirit's love and affection are set single-heartedly on us. He passionately yearns to fulfill His responsibility to the Father to help, teach, guide, and empower us.

James used the word *epipothei* to describe the Holy Spirit's intense desire to possess and fill us. The word *epipothei* emphatically means the Holy Spirit wants more and more of us. When it comes to you and me, He can never get enough.

I have walked with God since I was a young boy. Through the years, I have learned a very important truth about my relationship with Him: It doesn't matter how much I surrender to His sanctifying power today — by tomorrow He will be asking me to surrender more. Every second, every minute, every hour, every day, every week, and every year that passes by, my eyes are illuminated to new areas of my life that have never been surrendered, and He asks me to yield those areas to His control.

> After all the Holy Spirit has done in us, it should be no great shock to discover the Holy Spirit is in love with us. The fact that He views our mixing and mingling with the world as adultery should alert us to the intense love and affection He has for us.

During the altar call when I was saved, the congregation was singing "I Surrender All." Ever since that time, I've been on a journey to surrender all as the Holy Spirit convicts me and shows me areas I've never fully surrendered. I called Jesus "Lord" as a young boy many years ago, but I am still learning to accept His lordship in various areas of my life. It doesn't matter how much I think I've surrendered or how yielded I think I've become, there is always more to surrender and more He desires to possess of my life.

Likewise, the Holy Spirit desires to possess *you* — *all* of you. This desire is so intense that compared to natural, human lust, it appears almost excessive. He is focused on changing you, empowering you, conforming you to the image of Jesus Christ, and helping you fulfill God's plan for your life.

The amazing thing is that the Holy Spirit is in me and thinking of me, and He is in you and thinking of *you* at the same time. He concentrates on each one of us as if we are each His *only* focus. He is always looking for ways to help us in our spiritual journey.

The Jewish believers to whom James was writing were consumed with a lust for worldly possessions. And the Holy Spirit was consumed with a fiery, strong, passionate desire to fill up those Jewish believers with His love and affection. That's why it was so hurtful to the Spirit of God when they shunned Him and gave their attention to other things.

LONG-LASTING KINDNESS AND GRACE

Although the Holy Spirit can be grieved, He is not easily offended and wounded. He is not that fragile.

The Holy Spirit knows our frame and that we are dust (*see* Psalm 103:14). His mercy is great toward those who fear Him (*see* Psalm 103:11). As a father has compassion on his children, so the Lord has compassion on those who fear Him (*see* Psalm 103:13).

The Holy Spirit is full of long-lasting lovingkindness. It would take something very great to insult the One whose name is "the

Spirit of grace." Yet the Bible clearly teaches that when we discount Him, ignore Him, and treat His Word as unimportant in our lives, it grieves Him, and it eventually insults the Spirit of grace. *It is a serious matter to insult the Holy Spirit of grace!*

It's almost as if the Holy Spirit says, "After all I've done for you… I've given you My love. I've given you the new birth. I've sealed you, sanctified you, and empowered you for service. After I've done all of this for you, how can you so easily turn Me off and give your body, mind, and soul to other things?"

This is what grieves the Holy Spirit.

What area of your life is God dealing with you about right now? What area of your life do you need to surrender to the Holy Spirit? Is your tongue under His control? How are your attitudes? Are you surrendering your thought life to the Lord? How about your finances? Are your spending habits and your giving under the control of the Holy Spirit?

Your answer to all of these questions may be, "Yes, I'm doing all I know to do to surrender to the Holy Spirit's leadership in that area." That is as it should be. So then you simply keep walking in close fellowship with Him. It won't be long before He speaks to your heart and reveals another area that needs to be surrendered to His sanctifying presence. There is great blessing in sustaining an attitude of utter surrender to the Holy Spirit's watchful keeping and care.

Let the Holy Spirit love you! Let Him control you! Let Him exercise His authority in your life! Let Him flood

> **Let the Holy Spirit love you! Let Him control you! Let Him exercise His authority in your life! Let Him flood you with His divine desire! Every intention He has for you is good, holy, and pure.**

you with His divine desire! Every intention He has for you is good, holy, and pure. There is truly no downside to your decision to surrender your life — your mind, your body, your family, your spouse, your business, your ministry, your actions, and your behavior — to the Holy Spirit.

The Holy Spirit "dwelleth" in you, and He "lusteth" for you. Meditate on what you've learned about just these two Greek words, and you'll come to understand in a deeper way why the Spirit of God will *never* be satisfied with a shallow fellowship between you and Himself. He permanently abides within you, and He passionately yearns to fellowship with you, help you, teach you, guide you, and empower you. The Holy Spirit desires true communion with you, and He loves you too much to allow *you* to be satisfied with anything less.

THINK ABOUT IT

The devil will do anything to short-circuit the power of a believer's union with the Holy Spirit. Satan knows from personal experience that man and the Holy Spirit working in sync with Heaven's purpose is the divine combination that no foe can withstand. But there is a greater potential enemy than the devil to the strength of your union with the Holy Spirit — and that is *you*.

How is that possible? If you ignore the Holy Spirit's promptings concerning things He wants you to do or areas of your life He wants you to change, you short-circuit your own intimate fellowship with Him. And if you continue to ignore those promptings, over a period of time, hardness of heart and self-deception can set in. By continually looking into the mirror of God's Word and allowing the Holy Spirit to show you areas where change is necessary, your spiritual walk will not be hindered or abated. But if you refuse to look, you will become your own worst enemy.

Have you made a determined decision to listen closely and adjust immediately when the Holy Spirit reveals to you what is necessary to keep growing in Him? What can you do to maintain that position day after day and stay sensitive to Him? One key can be found in your fellowship with other believers who have made the same determined decision concerning their relationship with the Holy Spirit. Mutual encouragement helps all involved cultivate an intimate union with the Holy Spirit that no devil or earthly opposition can touch.

CHAPTER EIGHTEEN

THE DESIRE
OF THE HOLY SPIRIT

*J*ames continued to write, "…The Spirit that dwelleth in us lusteth to *envy*" (James 4:5). In the last two chapters, we've seen how the Holy Spirit dwells in us and longs for us. Now let's look at the extra depth of meaning that the word "envy" adds to this verse.

This word "envy" comes from the Greek word *phthonos*, which is used frequently in literature from the New Testament period, so we know precisely what it means. The word *phthonos* means *jealousy, ill will,* or *malice*. This is jealousy so strong that it tends toward *malice* and produces *envy*. The young man who lost his lover feels jealous for his old relationship to be restored and most likely will bear malice in his heart toward the romantic bandit. He is envious of that relationship and wants it back.

By now James 4:5 should be clear to us. The Holy Spirit is a Lover. He is preoccupied with us. He wants to possess us totally and desires that our affections also be set on Him.

When we walk and talk like unbelievers and give our lives to other things, the Holy Spirit feels like a Lover who has been robbed. He feels jealous for His relationship with us to be restored. He has divine malice for the worldliness that has usurped His role in our lives. And He is filled with envy to see things put back the way they should be.

When you put all three words — *dwelleth*, *lusteth*, and *envy* — together, this paints quite a picture. The Holy Spirit is not a passive partner. He aggressively and actively pursues you and me. He fiercely wants more of us! When we give any part of ourselves to something else or to someone else's control, He wants to seize it and bring it back under His divine control. He even has malice toward our preoccupation with other things.

We live in the world, work in the world, and function as human beings in the world. There is no way to get around that. Jesus didn't pray that we would be removed from the world, but that we would be kept from the influence of the world (*see* John 17:15).

> **The Holy Spirit is not a passive partner. He aggressively and actively pursues you and me. He fiercely wants more of us!**

There's nothing wrong with going to work, buying a house, purchasing a new car, or enjoying new clothes. Those things are great and very needful in this world. They are not wrong unless they consume and preoccupy our thoughts.

Let's remember the fact that all kinds of things can preoccupy our thinking. Even ministry can so preoccupy our thoughts that we seldom think of the Holy Spirit or our relationship with Him! Yes, that seems like a contradiction, but it is very possible to be so involved in good works that we never spend time with the Lord, read His Word, or listen to what His Spirit wants to say to our hearts.

Sometimes it's just the cares of this life that pull us away from the Holy Spirit. We can get so busy — so committed to doing so many things — that it deteriorates our spiritual life. Amazing as it is, even good things in life, if taken to an extreme, can become adulterous in the eyes of the Lord.

Only the Holy Spirit knows how to balance us. And the only way He can speak to us and keep us in balance is if we open our hearts and spiritual ears to hear Him. That won't happen if we are not setting aside a special time to spend with Him every day.

This is my question to you: *What are your thoughts focused on most of the time?* On your job? On your ministry? On a particular person? On your favorite hobby? On your household chores? On your gardening and yardwork? On redecorating your house? The answer to that question will probably tell you what consumes you most in life.

You can work in your profession without losing your deep affection and sensitivity to the Holy Spirit. Don't lie to yourself and say you can't, because your heart knows you can.

You can be a great spouse and a dedicated parent and simultaneously grow in your relationship with the Holy Spirit. You know you can.

Don't ever tell yourself you have too much to do and can't spend time with the Lord. The truth is, most people do what they want to do in life. If having communion with the Holy Spirit is a top priority in your life, you will make time for Him. If communion with Him is *not* a top priority, you won't. It's that simple.

> **If having communion with the Holy Spirit is a top priority in your life, you will make time for Him. If communion with Him is *not* a top priority, you won't. It's that simple.**

**In light of all we've discussed,
you could translate James 4:5 to read:**

*"The Spirit, who has come to settle down, make His home,
and permanently dwell in us, has an all-consuming, ever-
growing, excessive, passionate desire to possess us — and He
is envious and filled with malice toward anything or anyone
who tries to take His place in our lives."*

I believe that says it all.

How To Make Your Heart Right With the Holy Spirit

Perhaps you've been reading this book and thinking, *I have
so much to learn about the Holy Spirit. I didn't know I was supposed to have this level of communion with Him. I didn't know the
extent of what it means to depend on Him as my Comforter. I didn't
understand the seriousness of grieving Him with my attitudes and
my misplaced priorities. I just haven't realized how important my
relationship with the Person of the Holy Spirit is!*

If that's you, you're in a great place today. You are standing at
the threshold of a whole new realm of God in your life. For you
right now, humility is the name of the game. That's why James
tells us, "But he giveth more grace. Wherefore he saith, God
resisteth the proud, but giveth grace unto the humble.... Draw
nigh to God, and he will draw nigh to you..." (James 4:6,8).

The proud believer who refuses to listen or draw near to God
with a humble, repentant heart will have a rocky road ahead. As
we learned in Chapter Fifteen, God opposes the worldly Christian. For that person, there's nothing but frustration in the future.
God will block his way in order to frustrate him and bring him

back to his senses. This divine response has the potential of eventually bringing forth much fruit, but it's a difficult and painful way to grow in the Lord.

But God gives "grace unto the humble." The word "humble" in Greek is the word *tapeinos*, and it describes those who are *lowly and humble of mind, willing to receive correction and change.* This is the very opposite of the person who is haughty, self-reliant, independent, and unrepentant. God's grace flows freely to the person who possesses this quality of humility.

Furthermore, James promises that if we draw closer to God, He will draw closer to us. God and a repentant heart attract each other just as the opposite sides of two magnets are inevitably drawn together. As the humble Christian recognizes the need to change and draws closer to God, God Himself draws closer to that person.

The Holy Spirit comes to *stay* once He indwells the heart. We do not "draw nigh" to have the Holy Spirit — we already have Him inside of us. This drawing nigh to God is our first step toward entering into intimate communion with Him through the Holy Spirit.

I can't help but wonder how many Christians will die and go to Heaven, only to find out all they missed because they never experienced the communion of the Holy Spirit. Don't let that be your story!

The apostle Paul prayed, "The grace of the Lord Jesus Christ, and the love of God, and the communion of the Holy Ghost, be with you all. Amen" (2 Corinthians 13:14). That "amen" in Greek

> **I can't help but wonder how many Christians will die and go to Heaven, only to find out all they missed because they never experienced the communion of the Holy Spirit. Don't let that be your story!**

means *so be it!* Paul was not just praying a sweet-sounding prayer with no substance designed only to be stuck at the end of an epistle. No, the apostle really *meant* what he prayed! Thus, he concluded all that he had written by the Spirit in his epistle by saying, *"Amen! So be it!"*

Likewise, my prayer for you is that your spirit is stirred to press deeper and to move upward in your relationship with God. I pray that you will come to know the intimacy, the partnership, and the responsibility of the Holy Spirit in your life.

This is the secret place in God that I first began to discover in 1974 as a result of attending that Kathryn Kuhlman miracle service on the campus of Oral Roberts University. I can look back and say that was my starting place for a new and wonderful relationship with the Spirit of God.

If you have yet to embark on that same journey, I pray that this book will be your own starting place. Amen! So be it in *your* life!

The grace of the Lord Jesus Christ, and the love of God, and the communion of the Holy Ghost, be with you all. Amen.

— 2 Corinthians 13:14

Think About It

Jesus said, "…Occupy till I come" (Luke 19:13). Before you can fulfill that divine commission in the world around you, the first territory that is yours to possess and occupy is your own life. Your life may be full of many good pursuits. But if you are pre-occupied with any other focus besides Jesus, you run the danger of crowding out the space that is His alone to occupy. The Holy Spirit dwells within you to reveal Jesus to you and conform you to His image. He is utterly faithful to do His part. Your part is to clear out the distractions and allow Him to fully occupy His rightful place in your life.

Take the time to honestly evaluate what has been the dominant focus of your thoughts and attention over the past months and even years. Do what you must in the days ahead to make needed adjustments as you pursue a deeper communion with the Holy Spirit. That is the sure way *and the only way* to ensure that your life is a sustained demonstration of supernatural blessing and fruitfulness as it becomes His to command.

PRAYER TO BE FILLED WITH THE HOLY SPIRIT

The baptism in the Holy Spirit is a free gift to *everyone* who has made Jesus Savior and Lord of his or her life (*see* Acts 2:39).

After you made Jesus your Lord at the time of the new birth, the Holy Spirit came to live inside you and your old, unregenerate spirit was made completely new. This subsequent gift is the "baptism into," or *an immersion in*, the Holy Spirit. The baptism in the Holy Spirit supplies the supernatural power of God for witnessing about Christ, for enjoying a deeper, more intimate relationship with the Holy Spirit, and for victorious, powerful Christian living.

Receiving this precious gift is easy. Before you pray to receive it, you might want to read and meditate on the Scripture references I provide on the next page. Then expect to receive *the moment* you pray!

If you would like to be baptized in the Holy Spirit and speak with new tongues (*see* Acts 2:4), simply pray the following prayer and then act on it!

> **Lord, You gave the Holy Spirit to Your Church to help us fulfill the Great Commission. I ask You in faith for this free gift, and I receive right now the baptism in the Holy Spirit. I believe You hear me as I pray, and I thank You for baptizing me in the Holy Spirit with the evidence of speaking with a new, supernatural prayer language. Amen.**

As a result of praying this prayer, *your life will never be the same!* You will have God's power working through you to witness, to operate in the gifts of the Holy Spirit, and to experience Jesus' victory as a living reality every day.

Rick Renner

Scripture References for Study and Review: Mark 16:17; Luke 24:39; Acts 1:4,5,8; 2:4,39; 10:45,46

REFERENCE BOOK LIST

1. *How To Use New Testament Greek Study Aids* by Walter Jerry Clark (Loizeaux Brothers).

2. *Strong's Exhaustive Concordance of the Bible* by James H. Strong.

3. *The Interlinear Greek-English New Testament* by George Ricker Berry (Baker Book House).

4. *The Englishman's Greek Concordance of the New Testament* by George Wigram (Hendrickson).

5. *New Thayer's Greek-English Lexicon of the New Testament* by Joseph Thayer (Hendrickson).

6. *The Expanded Vine's Expository Dictionary of New Testament Words* by W. E. Vine (Bethany).

7. *New International Dictionary of New Testament Theology* (*DNTT*); Colin Brown, editor (Zondervan).

8. *Theological Dictionary of the New Testament* (*TDNT*) by Geoffrey Bromiley; Gephard Kittle, editor (Eerdmans Publishing Co.).

9. *The New Analytical Greek Lexicon*; Wesley Perschbacher, editor (Hendrickson).

10. *The Linguistic Key to the Greek New Testament* by Fritz Rienecker and Cleon Rogers (Zondervan).

11. *Word Studies in the Greek New Testament* by Kenneth Wuest, 4 Volumes (Eerdmans).

12. *New Testament Words* by William Barclay (Westminster Press).

ABOUT THE AUTHOR

 **Rick Renner** is a prolific author and a highly respected Bible teacher and leader in the international Christian community. Rick is the author of more than 30 books, including the bestsellers *Dressed To Kill* and *Sparkling Gems From the Greek 1*, which have sold more than 3 million copies combined.

In 1991, Rick and his family moved to what is now the former Soviet Union. Today he is the senior pastor of the Moscow Good News Church and the founder of a large media outreach that broadcasts teaching from the Bible to countless Russian-speaking and English-speaking viewers around the world via multiple terrestrial stations, satellites, and the Internet. He is also the founder of RENNER Ministries, based in Tulsa, Oklahoma. Rick's wife and lifelong ministry partner, Denise, along with their three sons — Paul, Philip, and Joel — and their families, lead this amazing work with the help of their committed leadership team.

CONTACT RENNER MINISTRIES

For further information
about RENNER Ministries, please contact
the RENNER Ministries office nearest you,
or visit the ministry website at
www.renner.org.

ALL USA CORRESPONDENCE:

RENNER Ministries
P. O. Box 702040
Tulsa, OK 74170-2040
(918) 496-3213
Or 1-800-RICK-593
Email: renner@renner.org
Website: www.renner.org

MOSCOW OFFICE:

RENNER Ministries
P. O. Box 789
Moscow 101000, Russia
+7 (495) 727-1467
Email: partner@rickrenner.ru
Website: www.rickrenner.ru

RIGA OFFICE:

RENNER Ministries
Unijas 99
Riga LV-1084, Latvia
+(371) 780-2150
Email: info@goodnews.lv

KIEV OFFICE:

RENNER Ministries
P. O. Box 300
Kiev 01001, Ukraine
+38 (044) 451-8315
Email: partner@rickrenner.ru
Website: www.rickrenner.ru

OXFORD OFFICE:

RENNER Ministries
Box 7, 266 Banbury Road
Oxford OX2 7DL, England
+44 (7522) 443955
Email: europe@renner.org

SPARKLING GEMS FROM THE GREEK 1

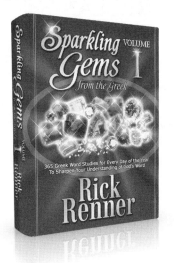

In 2003, Rick Renner's *Sparkling Gems From the Greek 1* quickly gained widespread recognition for its unique illumination of the New Testament through more than 1,000 Greek word studies in a 365-day devotional format. Today *Sparkling Gems 1* remains a beloved resource that has spiritually strengthened believers worldwide. As many have testified, the wealth of truths within its pages never grows old. Year after year, *Sparkling Gems 1* continues to deepen readers' understanding of the Bible.

$34.97 (Hardback)
1,048 pages

To order, visit us online at: **www.renner.org**

Book Resellers: Contact Harrison House at 800-888-4126 or visit **www.HarrisonHouse.com** for quantity discounts.

SPARKLING GEMS FROM THE GREEK 2

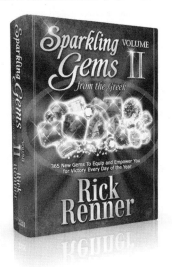

Now Rick infuses into *Sparkling Gems From the Greek 2* the added strength and richness of 13 more years of his own personal study and growth in God — expanding this devotional series to impact the reader's heart on a deeper level than ever before. This remarkable study tool helps unlock new hidden treasures from God's Word that will draw readers into an ever more passionate pursuit of Him.

$49.97 (Hardback)
1,280 pages

To order, visit us online at: **www.renner.org**

Book Resellers: Contact Harrison House at 800-888-4126 or visit **www.HarrisonHouse.com** for quantity discounts.

WHO STOLE CINDERELLA?

In *Who Stole Cinderella?*, Denise Renner shows why "happily ever after" is not a gift for a selected few, but rather an art that anyone can master who is willing to learn. With genuine warmth and candor, Denise recounts the journey of her own struggles in marriage and the unique insights she learned along the way to attaining emotional health and happiness. Your life will be enriched by the biblical wisdom Denise imparts and the originality with which she sheds light on your path to *happily ever after* and shows you right where to begin again if you've lost your way.

Even if the clock shows "past midnight" in your marriage, don't give up on your dream of experiencing a happy ending. Cinderella and Prince Charming are not lost — they just need to be rediscovered *God's way!*

"This teaching, like precious pearls, has been obtained by diving into the deep to learn of God and His ways over the course of many years. It is yours for the reading — but believe me when I tell you that it has cost Denise extravagantly."

— Rick Renner

$14.97 (Paperback)

To order, visit us online at: **www.renner.org**

Book Resellers: Contact Harrison House at 800-888-4126 or visit **www.HarrisonHouse.com** for quantity discounts.

BOOKS BY RICK RENNER

Dream Thieves*
Dressed To Kill*
The Holy Spirit and You* (formerly titled, *The Dynamic Duo*)
How To Receive Answers From Heaven*
Insights to Successful Leadership
Jesus' Message to the Church of Pergamum**
    (Vol. 10 in the Light in Darkness eBook series)
A Light in Darkness, Volume One
Living in the Combat Zone
The Love Test*
No Room for Compromise, A Light in Darkness, Volume Two
Paid in Full*
The Point of No Return*
Say Yes!* (formerly titled, *If You Were God, Would You Choose You?*)
Seducing Spirits and Doctrines of Demons
Sparkling Gems From the Greek Daily Devotional 1*
Sparkling Gems From the Greek Daily Devotional 2*
Spiritual Weapons To Defeat the Enemy
Ten Guidelines To Help You Achieve
    Your Long-Awaited Promotion!*
365 Days of Power*
Turn Your God-Given Dreams Into Reality*
You Can Get Over It*

*Digital version available for Kindle, Nook, iBook,
and other eBook formats.
**Available only through the iBooks Store.
Note: Books by Rick Renner are available for purchase at:
www.renner.org

THE HARRISON HOUSE VISION

Proclaiming the truth and the power

of the Gospel of Jesus Christ with excellence.

Challenging Christians

to live victoriously,

grow spiritually,

know God intimately.

![Harrison House logo]

For all the latest Harrison House product information,
including new releases,
email subscriptions,
testimonies, and monthly specials,
please visit **harrisonhouse.com**.